DEDICATION

I dedicate this book to my parents who pushed and prodded me to attend college and who supported me in my academic endeavors.

Thank you Mom and Dad!

TABLE OF CONTENTS

Secrets

to Successful

College

Teaching

How to Earn A Great Living And Be A Great College Teacher!

_____

Jo Macek, MAT

Secrets to Successful College Teaching: How To Earn A Living And Be A Great College Teacher

Copyright © 2013 by Forever Publishing

ISBN 978-0-9891290-2-2

Printed in USA by Forever Publishing LLC

Forever Publishing LLC

Casa Grande, Arizona

www.foreverpublishing.net

Forever Publishing LLC

Independent publisher of fiction and non-fiction.

FOREWORD

Congratulations! You have picked up this book because you are considering teaching at a college/university. Or you are currently teaching in higher education and want additional insight as to how to be even more efficient at what you do.

This book is not a book which teaches learning theories. There are scores of education and psychology textbooks which address how adult students learn, how to manage classrooms, how to design a curriculum, etc. Rather, this book offers the practical wisdom that is typically only learned by faculty the hard way – on your own, by trial and error.

As you read this book, you will understand that the inside information it offers could only have been written by someone like Jo Macek. Jo has been on both sides of the higher education fence. She has been in administration, responsible to recruit, hire and supervise faculty. She has been and continues to be a faculty member for a wide variety of colleges and has broad experience teaching traditional classroom-based classes, non-traditional blended classes, and online classes. Her willingness and openness to take on new challenges positioned her to be asked to be part of the first cadre of instructors to teach online when that delivery method was first introduced at one of the higher education institutions she was associated with. She had to learn by trial and error as there was no book such as this at the time.

"Common sense is not common." A better phrase may be, though, "common knowledge is not common." For the better part of my career, I, too was responsible for recruiting, hiring and supervising. Currently an adjunct faculty member, I have often thought to myself, "Why don't they know this?" when other adjunct faculty ask what I consider to be basic questions. The answer is, "common knowledge is not common." This book offers that common knowledge in an efficient and fun question-and-answer format. If this book had been available when I was hiring faculty, I would have given one to every person I hired. If it had been available when I began my teaching career, it would have saved me a lot of time and trial-and-error mistakes.

If you are fortunate to work for an institution which assigns you a faculty mentor to shepherd you through you first teaching experiences, great. If you are fortunate enough to work at an institution where colleagues are willing and able to share their experience to help you become more efficient in your teaching career, great. If you do not have these in-person resources, however, you now have a powerful tool to give you the "inside scoop," **Secrets to Successful College Teaching.**

Happy teaching!

Roxanne Lopetrone

INTRODUCTION

I began teaching college classes 20 years ago. My only qualification was my master's degree. While I knew the subject matter, I was clueless regarding the best practices and methods of teaching college. I tried to find specific information about college teaching, but only found generalities or theoretical analysis. I wanted a "how-to" book with specific tips.

This book began when less experienced instructors asked me the same questions I asked years before. The attention, therefore, is not on theory but on the practical information I learned by teaching online and on campus. I organized this book in manageable chapters focusing on the key elements of teaching.

College teaching is a rewarding profession that contributes to the well-being and progress of a society - you are teaching and training the new workforce and new leaders.

Thank you for taking time to read this book. You can choose to read one chapter at a time, the book in its entirety, or skim to find the information you need.

Sincerely,

Jo Macek

GETTING AND KEEPING THE JOB

The first step in college teaching is getting hired. However, in today's job market with the increased emphasis on adjunct faculty, the potential faculty member must compete with full-time faculty, other adjuncts, and industry professionals crossing over into teaching. A job teaching at a college, especially adjunct teaching, is much different than being hired at a corporation. The adjunct faculty contracts for one class at a time - the teaching "assignment". This means that you must be on your toes at all times, or someone can replace you next term. Your department chair will not ask you to teach another class.

These are the tips I found helpful to me and to other potential instructors in looking for and keeping college teaching classes. Good luck!

1. <u>If you want the job - apply.</u> Do not let your lack of major, degree, or experience stop you from applying. If you apply, you might get the job; however, if you do not apply I guarantee you will not get the job.

Many disciplines can cross over and apply to other areas. Social science majors includes courses in history, political science, or possibly anthropology. Economics includes math and statistics. Management includes marketing, accounting, international business, computers, human resources, and more. Communication degrees may include media, English, speech, journalism, public relations, human resources, and more.

Include a list of your applicable courses, training, and workshops at could be beneficial to your future employer. Sometimes, an adjunct faculty who has a master's degree but who can teach courses in multiple disciplines is more valuable than a Ph.D. faculty who teaches in only one area.

Teaching experience must not always be formal on-campus college classes. Teaching experience can also include leading workshops or training sessions, training   employees,   mentoring,   or   tutoring. Especially   include   any   experience   with presentations to groups.

Likewise, experience must not always be "paid work." Volunteer activities, at your employer or other group, can provide you with valuable skills. If you coordinated your company's United Fund campaign, annual picnic, or softball team, make sure you include these skills.

2. <u>Research colleges to which you want to apply</u>. Become familiar with the academics and programs as well as the mission statement of the college.

Some colleges insist on collaborative learning groups, at others this is an option, and others prohibit group assignments. Be sure your teaching style and schedule fits what the college requires. Are you a lecturer or interactive? Colleges have their own "personalities".

The mission statement gives you information about the focus of the college. This might be religion, career oriented, scholarly -research, or other.

A technologically oriented college with many computer-type degrees will have technologically oriented students. This type of student body is different than the student body of a liberal arts institution. A traditional state college will probably have younger students than a commuter college that serves towards older, working adults. Know yourself and your style.

3. <u>Jobs are out there, you just need to look</u>. One of the most important aspects to finding a job is knowing where to look.

These days, social media is important. If you do not have a LinkedIn page then I suggest you get one. LinkedIn is a combination of online resume and social media. You can include your profile (information from a resume) and also connect with various groups of interest. These groups might be academic and professional – sharing of information and ideas in an informal format – or job seeking. Yes, LinkedIn has job search capabilities. I also suggest including a photo of yourself. Whether you agree or not, research has shown that a profile gets more "hits" if the profile has a photo.

Facebook is another social media tool – but the key focus here is social media. Keep in touch with your friends and family through Facebook but connect with your professional colleagues through LinkedIn. Also - this may seem obvious to some, but is news to others - clear your Facebook page when job searching. Get rid of racy photos and never post negative comments about former or current employers.

Use search engines focused on college faculty. These include: Academic360 , Chronicle of Higher Ed, Jobs in Higher Ed, Twitter, any professional organization to which you belong, "colleges and universities in the US". Key these into a search engine.

Do not end your search there. Try an internet search for: colleges and universities in your state, online colleges and universities, indeed.com, CareerBuilder, jobing.com, monster.com, and more. Contact your old employers, friends, and anyone else you know –this is your network. Make sure you spread the word that you are available and willing to teach. This is not a one time communication. Keep in touch. If you can tell your Facebook friends about your sick dog or your new recipe for lasagna, you can certainly tell them you are available to teach and your discipline.

4. <u>Focus and be specific</u>. If you apply through one of the general job sites as listed above, you will be competing with hundreds or perhaps thousands of potential candidates. Make sure you distinguish yourself from the other candidates.

Review their college catalog. Review the courses you believe you are qualified to teach. Include these specific courses in your cover letter or resume. This shows that you know about the college and made a commitment to become aware of their curricula. I make sure I list college courses in my cover letter and how my experience ties in with this college. However, do not go overboard. If your degree is in biology, do not request to teach history. Tailor your resume to the institution.

Some colleges request a copy of your transcripts when submitting an application. I go a step further, I submit a list of my coursework divided into subject and graduate/undergraduate and institution. This may seem redundant since you will probably send a copy of your transcript later, but by sending a list of your courses, you make the job of the department chair (or human resources) easier. When sifting through 1,000 or more resumes - believe me - easier is better.

Direct your application and/or cover letter to the person who is hiring; this is usually the department chair. Go to the college website to find the name of the department chair and submit your resume directly to this person. You might be asked to submit to HR (human resources), but you have the name of a human contact for future resumes.

If an online website/job site requests specific experience, make sure you include these words in your cover letter and/or resume. Large employers who post jobs through large job sites (i.e. CareerBuilder) sometimes use filters to sift through potential candidates. The filters are key words in the job description. If the job posting states that the candidate must have experience in "developing syllabi", make sure you use these exact and specific words in your cover letter or resume. Do not make HR guess because they will not.

5. <u>Shine at the interview</u>. Whether your interview is in person or by telephone, you should be prepared to answer all questions.

You should have personalized your resume to the institution with pertinent education, experience, publications, etc so you should have this particular resume and cover letter handy. In addition, you should also have your CV (curricula vitae – "life story") available because this usually has more detailed employment information. If you have not practiced the "standard" interview questions then you should do so.

If your interview is by telephone, make sure you are in a quiet location. Do not have barking dogs, crying children, or loud music/television playing in the background. This is an indicator of your commitment to your students.

Write a few potential scenarios about teaching and problems with students and have these handy. Typical questions include:

How would you handle a student who plagiarized a paper?

How would you handle a disruptive/loud/obnoxious student in class?

What if a student could not meet during your office hours ? (due to student work schedule, for example)?

How do you handle student use of cell phones in class?

6. Apply often. Do not cross a college off your list just because you are initially rejected.

The college may not be hiring at the time, or have an excess of applicants, or have another candidate in mind already (but posts the position anyway), or fishing to see who applies. Applying when a position is posted means you are competing with all other applicants. Applying periodically may get your resume to the department chair at just the right time.

I maintain a list of colleges and dates of application. Periodically, I submit an application by mail or online to the college. But not too often as to be a pest.

7. <u>Once hired, be sure to attend faculty meetings and college professional development activities.</u>

> On-ground and online colleges have faculty meetings. These might be held on campus but with a video/audio/weblink conferencing component. Attending meetings lets you network with department heads, administrators, and faculty schedulers. This also shows your interest in the institution and being part of the academic team. Attending the college's professional development activities (online in synchronous or asynchronous formats) shows department chairs that you are committed to the college and also keeps you aware of the college's policies.

> Keep aware of the development activities required by your college. These activities are usually presentations or in-services and often include the annual harassment and/or discrimination policy, FERPA (Family Education Rights and Privacy Act), or university policy update. These might also be new methods of instruction (new technology), how to grade papers, including critical thinking into courses, etc. Usually these activities or in-services require a few hours or less and you might get a nice certificate of completion.

8. <u>Document and keep a file of your professional development activities</u>. Most colleges require that faculty submit an annual updated CV or resume. This is usually required for accreditation. The more developmental activities you attend, the better you and your college look to any accreditation agency. Also, many of your professional development activities may carry over to many different colleges.

> Keep files or documents by college. This can be a paper file or computer file. You can scan paper certificates to keep these in a computer file for easy access. This may be redundant, but is easier to retrieve and send when needed. In addition, send a copy of certifications or documentation to your department chair to keep him/her aware of your ongoing activities. I keep a list of development activities, staff meetings, conferences, and professional organizations sorted by college. When I am asked for an annual self-evaluation or update, I can copy/paste to the college's form. I also use this method to make sure I meet the annual development activities standard for the college.

> Keep an up-to-date CV or master resume with your experiences, jobs, volunteer activities, etc

9. <u>Publish/present at conferences.</u> Publishing and presenting are a plus on your CV and are required at some institutions.

Publishing and presenting are not as difficult as you may believe. Publishing might be a book review, an essay about your teaching experiences, or case study in a trade magazine or journal. Think about co-authoring an article a journal – one researcher, one literature reviewer, for example.

Presentations can take many forms. This can be a panel discussion, PowerPoint presentation, roundtable, or poster presentation. A panel discussion and roundtable gathers a few subject matter experts and moderates a topic discussion. For a poster presentation, make a tri-fold or bi-fold poster (available at an office supply store) of a case study, survey, or other information. Virtual conferences as well as webinars are becoming popular due to increasing budget constraints. You can log into a website and participate with others linked by the internet.

There are many hardcopy as well as online magazines and journals. Do an online search for "academic journals - (discipline)" or "trade magazine - (discipline)". Try your professional organization for journals publications. You can also join a listserv administered by a university; the listserv is a subject specific information group that posts upcoming conference, request for journal submissions, and available jobs without the chatter of a social online group.

I keep a file with potential conferences and journals. I cannot attend all of these, but I can plan for possible future presentations.

10. <u>Join professional organizations.</u> Most colleges require membership in a professional organization. This organization usually deals with the subject matter you are teaching. An example is the American Psychology Association (APA) for psychology, counseling, therapy, etc.

Large national organizations (APA for example) can be prestigious but also expensive, especially if your college does not pay for membership fees. Annual dues for some national organizations can be $250 or more. This can be expensive if you belong to several organizations. If you are not sure of organizations to join, ask your department chair.

Smaller state or regional organizations usually have lower fees and also may offer more opportunities for presentations and publications. The organization also lets you know about legislative issues, trends, development opportunities, and credentialing (if necessary).

11. <u>Know your time commitments.</u> Teaching is not something to be taken lightly in a few spare minutes of your time here and there. You are dealing with people's lives; they look to you for knowledge, guidance, and assistance.

If you do not have the time to devote to a class, then do not accept the assignment. Classes require time in preparing syllabi, lectures, online discussion questions, grading papers, formulating questions and responses to student answers.

Students know when instructors have not devoted time to a class – lectures are haphazard with old material, online replies are brief and address only the minimal number of students. If you have ever taken a class from an instructor who used "yellowed notes" (the pages of notes are so old that they have become yellow), you know these instructors are not current in theory, methodology, or information.

Preparing for a class involves time. If you develop the class based upon course objectives, you must choose a text book and/or readings; write your lectures; compose your presentations (i.e. PowerPoints); develop discussion questions; find ancillary websites that support research; finding YouTube videos, videos, DVD's; develop student learning activities; exams and quizzes; possible guest speakers or field trips; or other activities. This might take 40, 50, 60 or more hours. Developing a class becomes easier with experience, but still requires an investment of your time.

If you are an instructor for a class in which the curriculum is pre-set, then the course development does not take as much time. However, you still must read the textbook; find ancillary material including websites, YouTube videos, videos, or DVD's; develop ancillary presentations, lectures, discussions questions, or exercises. This might take 20, 30, 40, or more hours.

Once the class is developed, I usually allot one hour per day per online class, not including time for grading papers. With more experience in teaching online, I reduced the time I need but not the quality of replies. I usually allot about 6 to 8 hours for grading a 2 to 3 page paper for a class of about 25 to 30 students. This time allotment is not set in stone but is a general time frame.

12. <u>Forget week-ends off (and holidays!).</u> For online classes, most assignment deadline dates are on week-ends and initial discussion posts during the week.

> Therefore, most questions about assignments will be during the weekend as will questions about discussions for the week. This will probably be your busiest time.

> I usually check class email in the morning then again in the afternoon or evening. A few hours for a student can be the difference between a mediocre paper and a great paper or no paper at all.

> This certainly does not mean you will live in front of your computer. However, half an hour or so checking emails can greatly help your students with those last minute questions and will endear you to students because you will stand out from the instructors who do not answer emails on week-ends.

> A note about holidays: For me, personally, holidays are usually "down time" when I do not have anything else scheduled except family gatherings so this is a great time for me to log in to answer a few email questions or postings. I do this while the

turkey is roasting in the oven and before I assemble the green bean casserole. On the other hand, I hold some holidays as sacred and do not access the computer. In these instances, I make sure I schedule computer time into my week so I can check my online classes the day before and day after the holiday.

13. <u>You will probably spend twice as much time the first time teaching a class at any institution.</u> Even if you taught that course elsewhere. You want to make sure that your syllabi, lectures, questions, and assignments conform to the university's course objective. You need to read the text, or find the text, research ancillary materials, develop or modify lectures or presentations, etc.

14. <u>Try not to turn down classes.</u> As a former university administrator who scheduled classes, if an instructor tells me "no" a few times, I get the hint and do not contact that person for future classes.

If you wonder why a school has not contacted you, it might be because you said "no" a few times. Call or email the school and speak with the faculty scheduler and say you are available. This would also be a good time to inform the college of any new degrees, certifications, or preference for courses.

Of course this does not mean you should accept all courses offered. Take classes for which you are qualified.

My schedule is flexible so I can accept day, evening, or online classes. I tell my deans and faculty schedulers my availability and have taken some last minute assignments when a scheduled instructor had to withdraw from that teaching assignment.

15. If you feel isolated in your home office, spend time in location with other people buzzing about.

Spend an hour or two sipping coffee at a coffee shop, or other place with an internet connection. A new setting can be relaxing as well as stimulating. Have some coffee, sit back, enjoy your freedom as an independent scholar/instructor who is not locked into office hours or a cubicle. Do some people watching. You might become inspired with a wonderful new lesson plan or discussion thread.

I like to get away to a Barnes & Noble with Starbucks or our local library with Wi-Fi and coffee shop. I can relax, get away from home (spouse, dogs, etc) and browse for magazines or reference books. Sometimes I engage in an interesting conversation with another patron.

16. Be proactive in requesting teaching assignments. Check the schedule for upcoming courses and ask your dean or faculty scheduler about teaching these. Be aware of course and curriculum changes and possible future courses. If you have not taught for an institution for a few months, contact your dean or faculty scheduler. Colleges have different timelines to offer teaching assignments, and different requirements and limitations on adjunct teaching. Some colleges limit the number of classes taught concurrently or the number of classes in a year.

17. Deadlines are important. Just as you -the faculty- have deadlines for your students, your college has deadlines for you. If your college has deadlines about submitting syllabi, mid-terms grades or final grades, make sure you follow these.

Deadlines are not just college rules, deadlines are often federal regulations. This is especially true of attendance and final grades. Students who do not attend (or post online) might not be eligible for financial aid; therefore, cannot pay for the class. The college policy may require that you notify the appropriate department about no-shows. The student will probably be dropped from your class. While one less student may seem great to you (less papers to grade) this is not in the best interest of the college or the student. Students and the institution receiving federal financial aid must meet specific attendance requirements; the ramification is that financial aid monies will not be released to the student (and therefore the college.) Likewise, final grades are important not just for advancing to the next class but for standards of academic progress. If you do not know what SAP is or why it is important –then you should. SAP is the calculation of passing/not passing classes for potentially receiving or not receiving money to attend your college – this is standards of academic progress. College attendance affects enrollment which in turn affects the courses offered and therefore your job.

Something else to think about: If your department chair or faculty schedule is always having problems with you submitting your syllabus, your grades, or other paperwork, then why should that chair offer you a class if someone just as qualified and just as efficient is willing to comply with college rules is available?

18. <u>Address any deficiencies in evaluations.</u> Student and department evaluations are in place to help faculty members, not to criticize. Students provide anonymous feedback about your teaching style, student interactions, and command of technology. Department chair/colleague evaluations (critiques) provide you with information about your teaching style and opportunity to expand subject matter expertise.

> Use this feedback to improve yourself, and therefore keep or get teaching assignments. Some faculty panic and believe this is the opportunity for students to retaliate for a bad grade (which the student rightfully earned). . Chairs and administrators know that some students think they can "get back" at an instructor by rating an instructor as "poor". One "bad" student evaluation out of 20, 30, or more students will not influence your department chair

> Instructor and student interaction has synergy. Sometimes the mix of students and instructor personality does not lend to a positive experience for everyone involved. One bad class evaluation will probably mean a meeting (or phone call) from your department chair, but if all of your other evaluations have been stellar then this class is probably an aberration. Remember that your department chair's job is to make sure that all is going well in the class

and if an instructor has had some issues during the class then s/he would like these issues resolved before the next class begins.

As a former department director, I always appreciated faculty who communicated any issues they had that affected their class. This might be personal issues including work conflict for adjunct faculty or problem student(s). This gives us the chance to problem-solve.

The key to evaluations is to interpret the trend of feedback from students. Are students consistently stating that you are monotone in your lectures? Are students consistently stating that you are inconsistent in grading? Do not focus on one class. Think about your actions over several classes. Use these evaluations. Approach your department chair about attending conferences in the use of technology or ask for a graduate/teaching assistant to help grade papers.

As a final note: No one is perfect. Focus on the many positives, not on the one negative.

FINANCES

I am not an accountant or financial advisor (and I do not play one on TV!).   I do not pretend to know all about tax shelters, tax deductions, or other financial details. Only you are responsible for your finances and taxes – just as I am for mine. That stated, the following is what I have learned and used from my 20 years of full-time and part-time teaching and communications with my own accountant about my own taxes.

1.   <u>As with any financial or tax information from anyone, anywhere, at any time – ask your financial advisor or accountant</u>. You might receive great advice from a colleague, friend, relative, etc that sounds great but which might be wholly inappropriate for your situation. Just because a tax deduction was great for your brother-in-law in 2005 does not mean this tax deduction is still valid in the current year and not in your specific situation.

> I have had an accountant complete my taxes for the past 25 years. Personally, I believe my accountant is worth every penny. Each year I ask questions about what I can and cannot deduct and where I can or should put my hard earned money regarding IRA's, tax shelters, deductions and so forth. I pay my accountant for his expertise – just as your students pay for your expertise.

2. <u>Part-time employee v. independent contractor (self-employed)</u>.

Some colleges contract teaching services and pay as independent contractor. You should not need to do anything special for the college – in other words, you do not need a tax ID number or to file as a business. The college will send you a tax form of earnings at the end of the year, just as with "regular" employee status. However, this independent contractor status means that federal, state, and Social Security taxes are <u>not</u> withheld. The onus, therefore, is on the adjunct faculty member to reserve a portion of his/her pay to send to the federal government at tax time. You must also pay your portion of Social Security taxes. If the bulk of your teaching is independent contractor, make sure you reserve part of your monies for taxes. Also, if the majority of income is as an independent contractor status, you should be filing quarterly taxes with the IRS. <u>Talk to your accountant.</u>

In a part-time employee status (even though this is sometimes called 'contract'), the college will deduct taxes and such and you will receive a W-2 in January. You are treated as a "regular" part-time employee but paid on a per course basis (or even perhaps on a per in class hour rate).

Most of my teaching assignments have been to colleges who "treat me" as a part-time employee so I do reserve monies for taxes. On the other hand, I know of other instructors who have taught as independent contractors and who had to pay big $$$ to the IRS because they did not pay their taxes quarterly or owed "lots" to the IRS (and state governments) in April because they failed to withhold taxes..

3.   <u>Maximize per class earnings.</u> Some institutions pay more when faculty reaches a certain status. Research the requirements at each institution; check the faculty handbook or ask your department chair for details. Maintain record of classes taught to track these requirements.

For example: Some colleges pay more per class after teaching a set number of classes (after teaching 3 classes in one year you might earn $100 more per class).   Other institutions might require a specific academic degree (Ph.D. vs Master's or Master's plus additional credits) for additional remuneration. Keep track of your courses taught as well as degrees earned.

Other institutions might increase your remuneration due to specific administrative or development criterion such as attend faculty meetings, conference, timely submission of paperwork (syllabus, grades), or student evaluation scores in order to earn additional monies.

At a certain college, my income began at $900 per class and is now $1,200 per class; I taught there several years and teach several classes each year.

4. <u>Find other opportunities to get paid by the institution.</u>

Some colleges pay a stipend for publications or conference presentations in which you include the institutional affiliation.

Additional remuneration might include mentoring or training a new faculty member, participating on a university committee, acting as a department head, interviewing faculty candidates, tutoring students, conducting in-services, etc.

Be proactive. Ask your department chair or faculty development office about possible opportunities for contributing to the institution. This is also a great way to network with your department head and other faculty or staff members and can lead to additional courses.

Do not limit yourself to your department; larger institutions need faculty for such committees as student activities, university environment, or student academic progress review. Keep a spreadsheet or list of your activities for each institution. Even if the college does not pay you for this committee work, you can include these on your annual review. And you will keep in touch with your colleagues - always a valuable networking activity.

I received $250 for my short book review published in an academic journal. This was helpful for me (gaining knowledge about the field and including this information in my lectures) as well as the institution (accreditation). At another institution, I earned $100 for mentoring a new faculty member. This entailed weekly monitoring of the new faculty, review of his syllabus, allowing him to teach my course a few nights, and providing feedback to the new potential faculty and institution. This was a great experience for me (!) and I gained another network contact.

5. <u>Ask the college to pay for memberships and conferences.</u> Some colleges will pay for membership in a professional organization, if you include your college affiliation.

Some colleges provide a small travel stipend if you present or attend a conference and include your institution affiliation. Conferences do not need to be national or international. State or local organizations are usually less expensive and within driving distance, especially if your college will not pay or has limited reimbursement. Regional or state conferences are valuable networking tools in addition to gaining and sharing information about your field.

This might also be a great way to combine vacation and work. Find conferences in places you want to visit then submit a proposal or poster session. If accepted, include your institutional affiliation. You can present, then spend the rest of the time sightseeing. A few years ago, I presented at a conference in another state. My air fare, attendance fee, and lodging were paid by my institution. My husband joined me for a few days and we made this a mini-vacation. Please keep in mind that my college did not pay for my spouse's meals or activities, only mine. And, I attended all other conference sessions.

Do not limit yourself to conferences in your field; consider such conferences as teaching, technology, distance learning, K-12 education, or other complementary areas.

Keep track of expenses for tax purposes or reimbursement. This should include attendance fee, mileage, meals, lodging, airfare, materials purchased, etc. If your college does not reimburse you for this, you may be able to use this as a tax deduction.

I have a spreadsheet of potential conferences and proposal submission dates and try to attend something each year. I bookmark professional organizations and belong to several listservs to keep track of requests for conferences and paper submissions. Of course attendance at conferences adds to your body of knowledge and you can include this in lectures and online discussions in your class.

I once presented and attended a local conference. The attendance fee was $50, however, my college gave me $250 because I included my institutional affiliation.

Some colleges require faculty to write grants requesting monies for conference attendance. Do this. Even if you do not get the grant, or perhaps may receive a partial grant, this will improve your grant writing skills as well as letting your department chair know that you are interested in gaining exposure for the institution and knowledge for yourself.

6. <u>Teach 1 or 2 credit courses</u>. Some larger colleges have formal orientations and preparation courses (study skills), workplace development, leadership, continuing education, etc courses that are 1 to 2 credits.

These are often taught by higher level faculty, but occasionally other faculty can get these plum assignments. The orientation courses are usually week-end, one credit courses that orient the student to the college. This might include finding departments on campus, study skills development, or exploration. A 1-credit course might not seem like much, but this is sometimes $100 or more of pay and you can mold new students coming to the college. Often, these new students remember you several years later as their first instructor or mentor. These courses will probably not require too much homework to grade; and this might indicate your willingness to teach a variety of courses for your college.

Study skills development courses are often taught by English or communication faculty and focus on students gaining the skills necessary to be successful in a fast paced college environment. These skills include time management, reading (SQR3), note-taking, APA or MLA format, research, and so forth. Not all students are well prepared for college. These courses are usually 2 or so credits and either count or do not count towards college credit requirements. These can be fun and worthwhile courses and you can really make a difference in a student's life skills. For larger colleges, these are often taught in the summer when full-time faculty are vacationing or researching. Let your department chair, or other chairs, know your availability, eagerness, and qualifications.

7. Develop your own 1 or 2 credit courses. You might have an expertise in a specific area that is too narrow for a full class, yet is valuable and needed in the workplace.

Talk to your department chair about developing a specific course. This would entail writing course objectives, perhaps finding a book or writing your own, developing learning outcomes, and more. While this may seem time consuming, your expertise will make this an easier endeavor than if you were not knowledgeable in the subject matter. In writing a 1 or 2 credit course, you can add "curriculum development" to your resume and also provide students with valuable information. If this course is successful at your institution, think about approaching other colleges regarding this class. Keep in mind that colleges are different and that all colleges have their own specific objectives and mission statements. You will not be able to take class "X" at college "Y" and use verbatim class "X" at college "Z". In addition, some colleges require that you sign copyrights to the college.

8. <u>Be familiar with tax deductions and expenses.</u> You do not need to be an expert in accounting, but since you are paying these taxes you should be aware of your own money. Some knowledge about deductions can help with asking educated questions of your accountant. You can check the IRS website for some general information about deductions.

These are some of the potential tax deductions to ask your tax professional about:
internet services (provider)
telephone (landline or cell)
computer desktop/monitor/laptop/notebook/iPad
    equipment: cables, keyboard, camera, webcam,
    speakers, USB drives, mouse, modem, printer,

paper , transparencies, software programs, etc

mileage to and from campus (if part-time) or other
   venue (for research or conference)

meals while on campus or at a conference

books or music or DVD's used for teaching

Subscription to professional journals and magazines
   used for teaching

attendance at conferences or lectures not reimbursed
   by the college (fee, hotel, airfare, parking)

memberships not reimbursed by the college

special equipment or clothing not reimbursed by the
   college (protective eye glasses/eyewear,
      uniform, shoes, stethoscope, calculator, etc)

certifications/licensures/courses/preparation courses
   needed in your profession

office equipment, supplies used at home: files,
   filing cabinet, desk, etc.

Check with your tax professional about the
possibility of using the home office deduction. If
the majority of your income comes from work-at-
home, then you might be able to deduct part of your
mortgage interest, utilities, home maintenance.

While you cannot deduct everything, you might be
surprised at the items which are considered to be

tax-deductive.   As always: consult your tax professional (!)

9. Keep track of your pay dates and earnings. If you teach as an adjunct in many different colleges, you will find that these all have different pay dates. Keep a note of the date and amount due to you on your calendar (or phone or spreadsheet or whatever method you decide upon).

> Humans make mistakes and your college payroll staff may have hundreds of faculty to process. Mistakes are easy to make. You do not want to be short changed because someone forgot to include your name on a payroll sheet. Some colleges pay 1/3 at the beginning of the class while some pay 2/3 of the pay during the first month of class. Some colleges pay at the end of the class while others divided pay equally throughout the class.

> I mark my pay dates for each class on my calendar. Only twice has a college erred in my many years of teaching. However, if I had not noticed the error, the college would not have corrected the amount and I would have been shorted a few hundred dollars.

> I have a spreadsheet of colleges and total annual pay earned.   This gives me a quick glance as to the

monies I earn at an institution. If you are very detail oriented, you might want to compile a time log and track the time spent for each institution. The $1,200 per class might seem great until you realize you are spending 20 hours per week on the class so your hourly rate dwindles to less than minimum wage.

10. Check possible benefits offered by your college. Some colleges offer life/health/dental insurance for adjuncts. While the college will probably not pay the full amount or close to what the college pays for full time faculty, this gives you the opportunity to have some type of medical coverage.

Colleges might coordinate with companies to offer discounts for such products as computers, cell phone service, restaurant discounts for meals, and so forth.

Some professional organizations offer group benefits to their members. Check the member benefits section of these organizations. Some credit unions offer their members benefits. Do a web search for your state for private insurances geared towards teachers. Some insurance carriers are specifically established for teachers or like professionals.

An institution might offer profit sharing, or retirement benefits. Some colleges offer reduced tuition for adjunct faculty. This might be helpful if you want to take a few courses to expand your knowledge or become more marketable to other institutions. You might even be able to earn another degree (bachelor, master, or doctorate).

ORGANIZATION

Whether you teach full-time, part-time as full-time, or the occasional class to supplement your full-time job or retirement, organization of your time and space is important. The scatter-brained professor is humorous to watch on television (the one who loses student papers or important research notes), but this person is not serving his/her students and certainly not him/her-self. Do you really want to spend an hour looking for a student paper on your messy desk?

1. <u>Keep a file or binder for each course.</u> This can be a computer file or a paper file. If you keep your information on a flash drive or computer, organize your files by college, then by course.

> Include a section titled "administration" to keep handbooks, important memos or other information, how-to's (submitting grades, grading rubric, etc). In each class folder, you should include the current syllabus as well as previous syllabi you used. You might find that want to use a prior reading assignment or paper assignment. Folders within each course should be divided by week. In each week you can include notes, presentations, activities, ancillary materials, listings or listing of links to videos/music/YouTube videos, and discussion questions and posts. For me, sorting weekly is much easier to find. This also allows me find and use

information/materials in one course in another or at another college. I can easily find a PowerPoint or activity I used in a class at a particular college, and then use this for another class at another college (with some modifications perhaps).

If you like the hard copy paper version, you can print and include in a three-ring binder. You can slip transparencies into plastic sleeves and keep these in the binder by week also. You can use a regular cardboard box for each to keep manila folders labeled by week. Place any hard copy articles or worksheets/handouts for the class in the week's manila folder. The material is together by week and easy to find. This is also handy when you need to copy materials for your on ground class that day/evening (or a few days before) because all materials are together. If you are super neat and organized, a snazzy 2 or even 4 drawer filing cabinet is great.

Keep a class roster either in your computer file or your paper file.

2. <u>Check your class roster before class, on the first day of class, and at the end of the first week.</u> This may seem to be too much work, but it will save you time and embarrassment. Sometimes,

you receive a list of students in your class that is one or two days old - in other words: not current.

Checking your roster before the first day of class will help you organize activities and perhaps divide students into groups if your class is small enough. If you assign students to groups based on the first roster you receive, then you will be wrong. Try to wait until you have the final roster. It is frustrating for students assigned to a group when 5 or 6 of the class members have dropped.

For online and hybrid (on campus meeting and also online discussions) classes, send a note before the first day of class reminding students about the class. Some students "forget" they are registered and will drop or they actually attend the first meeting.

If your school requires that you contact missing students, check the current roster to determine if that student is still registered. It will save you a phone call or email to the student, department or student services. It is embarrassing (and a waste of your time) to call the student only to find that he dropped yesterday but student services department or registrar neglected to inform you.

For on campus classes, you might receive weekly rosters that must be submitted to administration. Make sure you photocopy this after students sign in (or you take attendance) and before you submit. You can also make a photocopy before students sign in. This is a good way to keep track of attendance and any special notes about that session, i.e. "Mark not here next week" or "Susan late 30 minutes" or "Sam has Q about dates of Civil War". I photocopy my paper rosters then keep in a manila folder tucked inside the book for the class. I used to shred these sheets after the deadline date for grade appeals passes, but now I keep these in a file for a few months. Every once in a while student services or financial aid departments will ask about attendance for a student (because they lost the paperwork) and luckily I have this information.

For on campus classes keep a packet with syllabus, worksheets, handouts, etc., and other items discussed on the first day. Unfailingly, one student will show up at the second session and ask "Did we do anything important?" Give this student the packet. S/he cannot state "My instructor didn't give me that information," to administrators.

3. Organize your calendar. Use a calendar to note start dates, end dates, and assignments due. I use a computer planner rather than paper, I note the assignment and discussion by week. This is easy for me to see what I will be doing that week in all of my classes rather than trying to gather materials the night before or day of.

> For example: Week 1 begins on Monday, January 21 so the discussion and homework for the week is in Monday, January 21st's schedule. And so on and so forth.

> In teaching multiple classes at multiple colleges, I might have several assignments on a particular day's schedule. This also gives me a head's up if I need special equipment or materials or field trip form a few weeks in advance.

> By planning your classes and having information handy, you will have a good sense of your time available and can apportion your time for grading assignments, or for leisurely activities. This also makes sure that I am aware of the deadline dates for final attendance, grade submitting, and so forth.

> You are certainly not required to use this system, but I find that I am less stressed and more prepared when I know what I am teaching week by week. If you

have ever had an instructor who walked into class and changed the day's lecture because he forgot to get the movie (or speaker, or equipment) then you know what I mean. This does not reflect well on the faculty member.

4.   Develop a time schedule of work. Teaching allows great flexibility, especially online teaching. However, since "the boss" is not standing over your desk, you must be conscious of your time and conscientious in allotting enough time to grade assignments, answer discussion posts, etc. I plan my daily activities, and include time for online postings, grading, and research or preparation. When I had a full-time job and taught part-time, I blocked time in my calendar to answer discussion posts and paper grading. This would be similar to an appointment.

For example: Monday. 6pm to 7pm. Post week 3 to ABC College. Or Saturday. 8am to 10am. Grading XYZ final paper.

By setting a set time aside for each class and college, you can keep track to make sure you communicate with students for the required amount of for each college. You also do not want to be locked to the computer posting messages all day or grading all day on a nice, sunny Saturday while everyone else is at the beach or pool party.

At one point in my career, my full-time job was part-time teaching. I am an adjunct instructor for several colleges so I am not at a worksite all day. My schedule is flexible but I developed a schedule that allows me to maintain contact with students, meet college deadlines, and have free time for myself. For online classes, I send a weekly posting on Saturday or Sunday (if the class begins on Monday). I set aside time each morning to answer or post discussion questions and answer student email. I set a limit for each class – perhaps 30 minutes or replies to 6 student posts. By dividing time or number of postings, I spend a little bit of time each day and communicate with all students in the class. If I have 30 students in a class, I can respond to 6 each day and be completed in 5 days. Then I can not touch the computer or homework for one day without feeling guilty that I have not communicated with students and knowing I have met all college communication requirements.

For grading, I set aside a chunk of a few hours, usually in the morning, before I get to answer discussions. Discussion posts can be like email or social media – you want to keep posting and commenting and before you are aware a few hours has elapsed. For me personally, I prefer to work in the morning so my afternoon and evening can be free for other activities.

My schedule usually is something like this:

Monday: 8-10 am Discussions
Tuesday: 8-10 am Discussions. PM: Research for history class.
Wednesday: 8-10 am Discussions. 2pm Prepare for Thursday class.
Thursday: 8-10 am Discussions. 6pm on campus class
Friday: 9-11am Discussions. 1-3. Grade papers.
Saturday: 9-11am: Discussions/Send weekly note/ 1-3. Grade papers.
Sunday: check email/free

These are general times. Sometimes I take more time in discussions and sometimes less. This schedule also lets me shift grading to Thursday or Sunday if I have plans for Saturday. This also lets me check student emails regularly and respond with a quick note, even if I state "I'll check about this" regarding a student grade.

If your teaching is primarily on campus, I suggest to check your class email daily; if time permits, checking in the morning and evening is a good idea. Checking email should not take a long time; this should be no more than one-half hour. While this seems like too much work for an on campus class - especially because you see your students each week – answering student questions or fixing issues before they become problems will endear you to students as well as your department chair. In other words, your faculty evaluations will be outstanding.

Please note: If you have a full-time job and teach one or two classes during the terms, your full-time job probably (definitely!) frowns on you answering student emails for your part-time job at work. In this case, I suggest to answer emails before or after your full-time job. This should not take too long, about one-half hour. Please let students know your schedule of communication. As a former faculty administrator, I had to field student complaints about faculty who did not return emails or phone calls in a timely manner.

Your schedule might look different. Do what works for you as long as you meet college requirements and communicate with your students.

5.   <u>Do not be chained to your computer</u>. Students are not online 24/7, so you should not be either. Check email once or twice per day and post discussion questions forum at your allotted time. You can spend all day in front of the computer checking and re-checking emails and posts; a new post or email might pop up every hour or so. But, this negates the point of being online and having a flexible schedule.

6.   <u>Set aside a room for a "home office" or a space as your "workstation"</u>. Just as any other telecommuting job, set aside a room or part of room in your house specifically devoted to work.

This area should have a desk, chair, lighting, and computer. You should have proper office supplies: pens, pencils, paper, stapler, scissors, hole punch, binders, etc. Call this "my office." Having a specific work area puts you into a work frame of mind. Just as if you were "at work", set a schedule for yourself.

My home office has my desk, computer and printer, shelves with books, office supplies, and a CD player with my favorite Jimmy Buffet music (something I could not have in a traditional work environment). My reference books are handy, as are any other items I need.

7.   <u>Purchase equipment that makes your teaching and life easier</u>. If the majority of your income is teaching, especially teaching online, you need to have good (great) equipment.   Most colleges specify the computer and internet requirements for instructors. However, these are minimums.   To be efficient and effective, exceed the minimum.

Speed is important with internet connections. The faster your connection, the faster the download and upload (of papers, for example) and the faster you will be done for the day. Dial-up is cheaper, but you might spend hours more in front of the computer each week.

Bigger is better with screen size. I have two-23 inch (measured on the diagonal) monitors. I can grade a paper on one monitor, save and upload to the student on another monitor. I can research information on one monitor and write notes on another. All of this without opening/closing/ minimizing windows.

A free standing microphone may seem easier than a headset (and more comfortable) but with the headset you can stand up to grab a book or stretch and continue talking to students. Also, the quality of sound with a free standing microphone is not as good as with a headset because we often move and turn our heads when we speak; this makes your voice fade in and out I have both microphones, just in case one is not working and I use them for different purposes.

Webcams are installed with some computers. These are handy for face-to-face meetings or using a software platform that streams your live lecture with slides and webcam. Adobe Connect and Elluminate are examples. Caution here! If a student has a slow internet connection, the streaming webcam picture will be choppy and jerky.

A reliable color printer may not be a needed item, but a reliable printer is. You will print contracts and faculty credentialing forms that need a real, not virtual, signature. You might also print worksheets, study guides, or syllabi at home rather than trying to rush to campus to use their computer printer.

Software is vital for on campus and online classes. Whether you have a Mac or PC, the current or at least newer version of Windows and/or Microsoft Office will help in making the composition of your documents more efficient. A spreadsheet such as Excel is helpful in keeping track of grades and attendance for on campus classes.

I highly recommend a virus protection software program. There are many on the market including PC Doctor, Webroot, Norton, etc. Check with your computer expert or read reviews about these. Even if you do not have an online class, an occasional scan of your computer can identify malignant "infections." If you teach online or surf the net for any amount of time, think about scheduled maintenance for your computer that includes scans, defragging, and dumping cookies. If you are not familiar with these terms, then seek a computer professional. Defragging and getting rid of cookies will help increase the speed of your computer. Talk to a computer professional.

Voice recognition programs can be a useful tool in composing lectures, discussion posts, and grading. If you have a PC with Microsoft Office, a voice recognition software is already installed. Another popular voice recognition program is Dragon Naturally Speaking, although other programs are available. You speak commands into a microphone and your computer will comply. The voice recognition will also type your words into documents and emails. Very handy if your hands are full or your typing skills are at the hunt-peck level.

For on campus classes, my rule is one bag or rolling backpack/suitcase/container (this looks like a milk crate and some have locking tops) per on campus class. You can change weekly manila materials folders for each class. The rolling container is great for classes that require many bulky materials: illustrated or reference books; artifacts for history, humanities, arts; science or medical equipment including anatomy/physiology models, stethoscope (and such), etc. Rolling containers are also great for people with back issues or who are just plain tired of carrying an armload of books. Rolling containers/backpacks can be purchased at almost any office supply store (Office Max, Staples, Wist, etc) as well big box retailers (Wal-Mart, K-Mart, Target, etc) and sometimes cost only $15. My bags/containers are in my office and available (visible) for the classes I am currently teaching. I place extra bags/containers in the closet, under the bed, or other storage area.

8.   Maintain an all-purpose class supply kit.   For on campus classes, I have a pencil bag that contains supplies I might need for class.

This includes:

Pens - students forget and extra are always good

Mini-stapler with staples – I dislike looking for a stapler, only to find one in another room but without staples

Staple remover

Paper clips/binder clips – this keeps student papers together

Transparent tape

Rubber bands

Dry erase markers in assorted colors – Should the college provide these? Of course. In reality, often these are missing or dried. I keep mine in a clear plastic bag.

Dry erase marker eraser – this can be the authentic eraser or the old fashioned chalk eraser. I keep this in the clear plastic bag with the markers.

3 x 5 cards – you would be surprised how often you need these as placeholders, to ask for student

feedback, name tags, etc.

Post-it notes

Pop-up tabs – marking pages in books

Band-aids

9. <u>Keep a back up copy of teaching material.</u> One USB (or computer folder) should include your ongoing work: lectures, presentations, articles and so forth. A back-up USB should be stored in a safe location at home or work. Set a timetable for back-up, perhaps at the beginning of the month. This may seem redundant or unnecessary until you lose your drive or computer crashes or your computer files are eaten by a virus.

10. <u>Have a back-up plan in case your computer crashes, or you lose electricity or internet connectivity, or other emergency.</u> The stories your students tell you are sometimes true. Weather emergencies occur and unfortunately electric power or internet connectivity might not be available for days.

The saying is: "Plan for the worst but hope for the best." A contingency plan is always helpful in those rare instances when you may not be able to communicate with your online students for hours, or sometimes days. Locate an internet coffee shop, library, local college, or other location where you can relocate until power and such are restored. Many fast food locations now have free internet.

Watch out, however, because public libraries sometimes limit time for computer use. Other options might be a friend's house or colleague's house.

You might also be able to communicate with your students with a Smartphone. Keep your students aware of the situation.

This is my recent personal experience: Due to a squabble between the city and my internet provider, everyone who used this provider lost internet connectivity for about 10 days. I used my notebook computer (smaller than a laptop) at a local coffee shop and at McDonald's to maintain online discussions. I downloaded papers and graded these from my home desktop, then returned these to students at the coffee shop. Not the best scenario, but I maintained my level of communication. Likewise, several years ago after a severe ice storm, my electricity and internet were down for a few days. I was able to access my class at a friend's house a few miles away.

Have a hard copy of college emergency phone numbers available as a hard copy in a paper file (or in your smartphone) so you can keep them aware of limited access. If all of your information is on your computer, but you cannot access your computer you are out of luck as are your students. I have all URL links to colleges and college email written down just in case I need to access from another location.

11. <u>Keep student emails in a file until after the deadline for grade appeals.</u> Keep student emails separated by class in folders (online email in your inbox). This is especially helpful if a student – or your department chair - has a question or issue later in the term. You can also refer to these emails later if you or the student has a question. If this seems too organized, keep the emails then delete after the deadline date for grade appeal. The important point is to keep student emails until much after the class has ended.

BASICS

Whether you teach on campus or online, there are a few basic "common sense" protocols to follow. These are not etched in stone but are helpful in organizing, writing, and maintaining your class. These suggestions include tips for online and on-campus classes.

1. <u>Be familiar with the book</u>. This is your resource and reference for the course. Students refer to the textbook since this is their major source of information.

> For pre-set curricula courses, you should know the layout, information in the text, and examples you can cite. If you post information contradicting the book, your students will question you about it. This also means that you need to use the edition used by the college, and also to know the information contained in that edition. Make sure your information is valid, relevant, and up-to-date. You might also have a list of supplemental information that includes articles, websites, video/DVD's, or books that students can use for research or to gain knowledge.

> If you choose the textbook for the course, make the book is relevant and adds value to the course and is not just busy work. Texts should be current and conform to your (or college's) course objectives. As

above, students appreciate a list of suggested readings that add to the course.

Students also appreciate an economical book. Textbooks can cost $100 or $200 or more. For students who receive financial aid or who must pay their way with summer and part-time jobs, $100 for a book not referenced by the instructor or does not add value to the class is not only disappointing but unfeeling.

This applies to courses you might develop for a college to be used as pre-set curricula. I once had the unfortunate experience of teaching a humanities class using a book last updated in 1968 with photocopied (in black and white!) photographs and that had very ethnocentric viewpoints. You bet I complained to my department chair! Dated information is not fair to students and not good for your reputation – you should be current in your research.

2. <u>Conform to course objectives (learning outcomes).</u> This is the information students are expected to learn and you are expected to teach.

If you teach in a pre-set course, the homework assignments and readings were developed by an

SME (subject matter expert) and conform to the objectives. You "plug" your knowledge into the class with mini-lectures (i.e., guidance, weekly overview, objectives), ancillary materials, and discussion posts. This is also your opportunity to expand on the material for students through lectures, scenarios, activities, videos, and such. Focus on the objectives and make sure that evaluations assess the objectives for the class. In other words: How do you know students are learning what you want them to learn?

If you design your class, the objectives may be set by you or the college. Think about what is important for your students to know and accomplish – these are the course objectives (learning outcomes). When you design your course, think about each lecture, each reading assignment, each written paper, each activity, and how these relate to your course objectives. If an activity or a reading is not related to an objective, much as it may be interesting for you, it does not belong in the class. If you think a course can be thrown together at the last minute – you are just plain wrong and are cheating your students by not providing them with relevant and important information.

Remember that a course is designed based upon student learning (objectives), not around the textbook.

3.   Choose assessment tools well. An assessment tool provides feedback to you about whether students are learning the information presented through lecture, readings, assignments, and activities.

If you develop your course, you choose whether you will assign a paper, group activity, test, and so forth. Do not overload students with two or three or four methods to assess the objective. Just because you can include every assessment technique does not mean you should. Think about course objectives and how students can show they meet these objectives.

Each assessment tool should correspond to a course objective. Assessment does not mean graded assignment. As assessment can be an in-class group activity which you monitor. Or a unit (or day) non-graded pre-test/post-test. Or a series of discussion questions. Or ask students to write down the main idea/theory/what they learned on a 3 x 5 card to submit to you at the end of the class. These are formative assessments - assessing student learning while learning is going on. The formative assessment gives you feedback about how well you are teaching the material as well as how well students are learning the information.

Assessments let you know if your teaching method is getting through to students. This is more than right/wrong answers. You can develop – or use the college's – scoring rubrics. Scoring rubrics define the standard of performance for a student. Rubrics are used most often in scoring written assignments, especially papers. A rubric is helpful for students to assess their learning, and also for you to be fair in grading. (refer to Grading/Testing chapter)

4. <u>Stay away from graded group (collaborative) assignments, unless the college requires this or this is a course objective.</u> Group assignments are cumbersome for faculty and for students.

Students must communicate with each other or they must decide on a time to meet to discuss the project. By the time they have contacted each other and decided on a meeting time, one or more weeks have passed and a student or two has dropped the course. Then, you might need to readjust the group members. Also, students will want to meet during class time to coordinate the project and this will take from class time.

Likewise with online classes: Online students are not sitting by their computers 24/7 waiting to receive emails from their group members. In an online class, the assignment requirements must be established as soon as possible to allow students enough time to communicate with each other and to coordinate the their portion of the assignment. By this time, a few students have dropped or do not show for the class.

Grading group projects is cumbersome. Think about the effort of individual students as compared to the whole assignment. If the student who is assigned to complete part 3 of the project does not provide his/her piece, think about how this affects the entire group. Should an excellent student be penalized because a negligent student does not complete his/her assignment? If you require group assignments, be fair to participants who complete the work.

Some instructors use the rationalization for group assignment that the "real world" workforce requires team work, so college groups are a precursor of these. However, "real world" team work is much longer than a 5 or 10 or 15 week class and team members are assigned based upon their assessed skills rather than class roster.

This does not mean that group assignments or activities should never be used. I use short in-class group activities to demonstrate an idea and assess student knowledge. I sometimes use group assignments but assess individuals based upon their component of the project. If one of the course objectives is to be able to work together as a team then a group project would be appropriate.

5. <u>Stay away from online synchronous (real-time) activities, unless the college requires this.</u> In the online format, synchronous is a real-time lecture, presentation, or activity in which students listen and can participate from remote locations.

If the college requires one or more synchronous lectures, then students should be aware of the dates and times of your lectures. I teach for a college in which all lectures are synchronous with the dates and times scheduled like an on campus class. Students log into the course via weblink and listen to the lecture (and can participate) on their computers – wherever their computers happen to be. This activity requires a headset with microphone for listening and participation. While this sounds great –talking to students in real-time and they can ask questions in real-time – be aware of some complications with this platform.

Think about the following issues and how you would address these:

Internet problems – you or student cannot access the class

Computer problems - yours or student's malfunction of software platform

Microphone problems – your microphone is not working and students cannot hear you

Amount of "participation" by students – this format is primarily a verbal participation, not visual. Students cannot see each other, only hear the speaker.

How much participation is required? Must all students talk at least once? Talk at periodic time frames?

Noise is a distraction – from your location or the students' (usually student microphones are muted, but when unmuted everyone can hear the dog barking and babies crying

If the synchronous activity is an option, think about the issues of time coordination before you schedule this format. Students must be aware of real-time requirements during or before registration for your course. Also, this is a commitment from you that you must be at a certain place at a certain time. If you are in California but your college is in Indiana and students are scattered around the globe, you might need several time schedules to effectively communicate with your students.

6. <u>Do not use snazzy technology just to use the snazzy technology.</u> Okay, you attended that great "how to integrate technology into your class" conference and now cannot wait to show off your new skills.

Before using (and requiring students to use) that new up-to-date technology, think about the proficiency level of your students as well as their availability to the technology. If you integrate web 2.0, webcasting, or another technology, you must ask yourself the purpose. Are you showing off, or are students learning material? If you have an online or on campus class, do you need a blog or real-time synchronous activity or recorded Tegrity lecture?

Think about this: Students in rural areas do not always have the speed of satellite or cable and must use dial-up. International students in some areas face additional challenges of frequent electricity and internet connectivity interruptions.

This means that you must be aware of the student demographics of your college. Community colleges that cater to a local population may be okay with a synchronous activity or recorded lecture download as long as the students are urban, local not rural. An online for-profit college may have a diverse student base with international students or students living in various time zones. The key here is the student: How will you reach your student academically and make that internet connection?

I teach at colleges that use synchronous activities but about 20% of my students are international who must adjust their schedules (or I must adjust mine) to commit to a real-time lecture or activity. This means these student must be awake at 2AM for a lecture or discussion.

Other technologies might include PowerPoints, Prezi, YouTube videos, Jing, Skype, and more. These are presentation formats (PowerPoint, Prezi), video recording (Jing), and weblink camera (Skype). Think about the time you need to learn these technologies, whether your students understand these technologies, and the efficacy of these technologies in relating the course material to your students.

This does not mean that real-time online or recorded online technology should not be used. This can be a useful tool in which real-time discussion among students is vital to the course. This might be a science class discussing a project, critical thinking class discussing an issue, or business class discussing a case study. As always, think about the purpose of the technology and why this is important.

7. <u>Keep in contact with your students.</u> If a student has not posted in an online class, send the student an email. If a student has not attended class, send the student an email or call the student. Of course, this is viable in smaller classes, not lecture classes of 300 or more students.

You also want to be aware of your college's policies about student contact. Some colleges require weekly student contact reports. This is usually a federal student aid requirement regarding "attendance" or "contact". Send a brief note to your students who have not posted.

I send this short note to students:

"Hello, (student),

(course name and number) began on Monday, August 25. However, you have not yet signed into this course.

Please be aware of (name of college) policies regarding attendance. Also, please be aware of my late policies (insert late policy here).

If you want to continue this course, please contact me as soon as possible and we can discuss assignments and such.

If you do not want to continue in this class, please contact your academic counselor (or whoever is responsible at your institution)."

With this note, I sometimes receive notes from students who thought they dropped, but did not, students who 'forgot' about the class because they registered months ago, or students who had internet/car/family/illness issues.

This is often when you – the faculty member – have some leeway regarding student participation and attendance and you must decide if you will allow the student to continue or not. These student communications at the beginning of the course will avert the late course panics and communications from the student, your department chair, student services, and financial aid. Be proactive, this will endear you to administrators and save you headaches later.

8. <u>Develop your own "class."</u> Some courses have about the same content. These courses might include introduction to psychology, introduction to sociology, humanities, etc. Colleges may have different texts and different course objectives, but sometimes the material and objectives are very similar from one college to the next.

Certain facts do not change. Michelangelo painted the Sistine Chapel – this has been documented and will not change. You can use these consistent facts in your lectures. The same is valid with psychology or sociology theories. And biology and chemistry. The basic foundational theories have not changed so you can use this information in several courses at several colleges.

You might develop a lecture, PowerPoint, or other presentation based upon these foundational principles. You do not need to reinvent the entire class each time you teach the same subject. You might choose different texts for different colleges but the foundational material remains valid. This applies to case studies or content specific information. The text chosen by the college might not include your favorite case study but you can use the examples in similar courses.

I have a set of presentation slides that I can use in many different courses. These are general content slides to which I can add or delete information (questions, comments, examples, student activities, etc) depending upon the college and course objectives. This saves me time because I have most of the material at hand. As always, I make sure my information conforms to the college learning outcomes (objectives) for the course.

9. <u>Selling your developed course to colleges. Not!</u> In the early days of online education, some believed that skilled educators could develop their own courses and sell these to colleges for big bucks. A few decades later, we know this is not true. For-profit colleges do not depend upon the academic reputation of faculty and state or private colleges focus on course outcomes that align with college philosophies (not yours).

Individual colleges ask (contract) faculty to develop a course that aligns with their course outcomes. However, the contract usually stipulates that the course ownership belongs to the college, not to the faculty developer. This means that the college owns the course and their choice of faculty can teach this course. You - the faculty - are a contract employee. Another college will not "buy" your course unless you teach the class.

If you are pre-eminent in your field (published lots of books that are used by industry and colleges) you are probably teaching at a prestigious college and write your own courses for these institutions anyway. Or if you are a practitioner and expert in the field but not faculty, then you may not be knowledgeable enough about learning outcomes, methodology, and copyright issues to develop a course to sell.

Other, less prestigious faculty and colleges will have other faculty write courses that are owned by the college. Also, if you are thinking of selling in an online format, the online platform differs among institutions. Also, for-profit and non-profit colleges differ legally regarding use of such copyrighted material as movies and articles.

10. <u>Use your students.</u> They have a wealth of knowledge and experience. Ask students to share their experiences.

If you teach at a college with a predominantly adult student population, these students have a great deal of experience they can relate to the class. You can draw out student experiences and ideas by asking questions, organizing students into groups, or presenting case studies.

If your students are traditional (18 to 25 years old, living on campus, limited responsibilities), they have some experiences or pre-formed ideas you can use in activities. These can be guided experiences to get students thinking in different directions.

Students are not a *tabula rasa* (blank slate) but individuals who are willing to gain new knowledge and expand their thinking skills.

For classes in which my students are older, experienced adults, I pose questions on which they can draw their personal experiences. For classes in which students are younger and less experienced, I use case studies or examples to which younger students can relate.

11. <u>If you group students, do so based upon course objectives.</u> If your college or your course requires grouping of students in

various activities, think about the purpose of the exercise to draw the best performance and outcome from your students.

Grouping can be arbitrary, high and low performing groups, or high and low performing students together. The high performing groups will manage themselves to interact act accomplish the goals of the group. This will allow you the time to monitor and interact with the low performing group. With a diversity of skills in a group, the high performing students can guide the low performing students in accomplishment of group goals.

Grouping into high and low performing students is not a judgment upon student intelligence. Students bring many skills into a class. These might include technical computer skills (those who know how to compose presentations), presentation skills (comfortable talking to large groups), composition skills (writing and editing), time management, leadership, and others. If you know the skill level of your students, you can better decide to group them to achieve your course objectives. Think about what you want your students to learn from the grouping activity: team work, division of labor, leadership, presentation skills, technical skills, writing, etc.

12. <u>Use the book but do not teach the book</u>. Some colleges have pre-set curricula in which another instructor has designed the class; or perhaps you have designed your own class. In either case, include the text book material, but do not restate the text.

> In some courses, the textbook has been already chosen. In pre-set curriculum courses, the discussion questions and homework assignments are already written. Your job is to explain and expand upon the textbook and assignments with your subject matter knowledge by providing examples and clarifying difficult points. Students can read the book; you do not need to restate the same information. Use the book as a stepping stone to expand upon ideas and provide examples that illuminate a point.

> Students can pay $100 or more for a textbook. Include examples from the text or readings so students can refer to this information. If you have flexibility in assignments, assign homework from the book. A common complaint of students is that they pay lots of money for a book but do not use the book (do not have assignments from the book). Include information from texts in lectures, online discussion posts, or assignments. If you did not choose the text (and perhaps have a preference for another), do not complain about the text to the students. They are

probably not aware that the text is bad or good, and the text was chosen for a reason. If you cannot change the book, do the best you can with what you have.

If you choose the text(s) for your class, be considerate of students on a budget. Texts can cost $100 or more, perhaps $500 (or more) each semester for a full-time student. Students can better use money for gas, rent, or groceries. Not using a text, or only requiring a text because you read it in college, is a disservice.

13. <u>Be supportive but firm.</u> Students have many responsibilities and tugs on their time. They are working, have families, volunteer, and take classes simultaneously. Students might vent about the amount of homework or readings. Be supportive and understanding. Make students feel like the adults with responsibilities that they really are. Do not insult or put obstacles in front of your students. You are not helping students by being obnoxious, unkind, mean, or degrading. Students are people. Young students need guidance and older students need confidence.

You can be understanding and supportive without compromising your own integrity or the integrity of the college. Tell students you understand and empathize with their work, home, illness, etc situation but policy requires that you conform to deadlines. Or perhaps you will make an exception to the deadline. This is your choice. Encourage your students to continue in their studies. Setbacks are only in the short term.

Students can have challenges while attending college. This might include a death in the family, major illnesses, financial difficulties, computer or other technological issues, car troubles, and so forth. These situations occur to many people in real-world situations. What if your department chair were not flexible when you were late in submitting your syllabus because you had the flu? What if your computer crashed just before your presentation at your important conference? What if a large storm knocked down trees in your neighborhood - as well as the electricity - in your town? To tell students that you will not accept late work, or to quit their jobs to attend college is not helping students achieve their goals and not teaching them any worthwhile lessons.

This does not mean you must be a "mush" and give in to all student demands. You can be supportive while being consistent. Reinforce the need for proactive communication by your students.

Example: "Bobby, I understand you have overtime and are working 60 hours this week. I know that pay is important to you and your family. However, college policy requires that I do not extend the deadline date for this assignment. This is only one grade. I suggest you focus on future assignments and do the best you can for these. If you have questions, please ask. Hopefully, we can fix any issues before they become problems."

If you are steadfast in your deadlines, then be clear about this. State your policy in your syllabus. I suggest to underline, bold, and possibly even capitalize this.

Your policies might include any of the following:

All assignments due at midnight
No late assignments accepted
Assignments due at the beginning (or end) of class
Assignments submitted after class are late
No assignment accepted after 3 days late
10% reduction of grade for each day late
20% reduction of grade for each day late
Late worksheets (questions/case studies/graphs/
    problems) will not be accepted

Or any combination of the above. You might decide not to accept late worksheets/short assignments/reviews (especially if you have a large class and many are due throughout the term), but you are willing to accept late research papers (with a penalty perhaps?).

Review your late policy in class. In addition, provide all information needed for assignments in the syllabus and do not "surprise" students with changes in assignments. Just as you have a schedule to maintain; many students have outside schedules to complete assignments.

14. <u>If you do not take plagiarism seriously, then neither will students.</u> Students' copying the material of others is not a new 21st century phenomena. People have been taking credit for other's work probably since the beginning of recorded history. However, in academics, the use of another's work is tantamount to stealing and shows the character of the student, the instructor, as well as the institution.

Students might think that plagiarism is "no big deal". However, by taking someone else's words, the student misses a great deal of the education process. The skills student learn in writing papers include:

researching information from a variety of sources, developing critical thinking skills, focus and problem solving skills, and composing sentences and organizing paragraphs (organizing ideas). All of these are learned skills that students develop over time with trial and error experiences. Students are too often focused on the grade – the final product – while instructors are keen on the process. Include your (or college) plagiarism policy in your syllabus.

Plagiarism must be taken seriously by your institution – there are penalties for copying. You, the instructor, must also be aware of the possibility of plagiarism and have a specific plan when discovering an infraction. Be aware of your institution's policies regarding plagiarism and conform to this. Maintain your integrity. Guide students who are confused.

Plagiarism is not always clearly defined. Obviously, a paper in which only the writer's name is changed is clearly plagiarism. What about a paper in which a student copied but cited all materials – with almost no personal analysis? Is this plagiarism if the information is cited? What if 30%, 40%, 50% of the paper is copied? Or copied but cited?

Students with little experience in composing research papers (perhaps whose high school standards accepted copying passages from texts to answer questions) might believe that copying and citing is acceptable. Should this student be failed or given another chance? Depending upon your student population, you may need to review the definitions and examples of plagiarism. Not all students have the same level of experience and expertise.

Some colleges use such plagiarism detection software as Turnitin or SmarThinking. This might be a requirement or option for you or students. Include this requirement in your syllabus. I require students to submit papers through plagiarism detection software. If a student "forgets" or has problems, I submit the paper to the plagiarism site.

Most students are honest and do not plagiarize. Some students do not understand plagiarism. Some have time constraints and short cut papers by copying passages. A small number of students purposefully cheat.

15. Review the syllabus. Review the syllabus in class.

This review should include your course objectives, readings, assignments, and also policies about late homework, attendance, plagiarism, and communication. Give students the opportunity to ask questions. You might also want students to sign an acknowledgement form that they received and understand the syllabus. If you have a website for you or your class, a copy should be available for downloading just in case a student misplaces his/her copy.

In online classes, include a discussion forum specifically for syllabus questions. This is helpful to target answers and also students will not need to sift through other general questions. You might also include a graded quiz or assignment relating to your syllabus to ensure that students read the syllabus and understand the information.

16. <u>Be familiar with college policies</u>. These policies may be college specific or may be required by federal regulations. You do not have to memorize these, but you should have a contact list handy (online or on paper) or some general guidelines about possible issues that might arise. <u>Check with your college dean or administration!</u>

1. FERPA: Federal Education Rights and Privacy Act concerns regulations concerning student and institution confidentiality and records disclosure. I

suggest that any information you want to disclose is fielded through your college (e.g. disclosing grades) Check with the ADA department/representative or your college or dean)

2. ADA: Americans with Disability Act has to do with accommodations for students with disabilities. This might include additional time for assignments. Check with your ADA office/officer Check with your dean If a student requires an accommodation, you are usually notified of the requirement prior to the beginning of class, or during the first week.

3. Sexual harassment or Discrimination. Understand what constitutes harassment and/or discrimination at your campus and the contact person or department.

4. Financial aid: attendance requirements

5. Alcohol/drugs/guns on campus: phone number to security or emergency number, and policies regarding such issues

6. Dress code: yours and students

7. Cell phones in class: college policy (if applicable)

8. Food or beverages in classrooms: college policy (if applicable)

9. Disruptive behavior: phone number to security or emergency number, policies regarding such

10. Academic issues of students: services available including tutoring, writing center, academic advising, etc.

17. <u>Cell phones.</u> Your college may or may not have a policy about cell phones in class. Include your policy about cell phones in your syllabus. Check with your administrators about college policy, if any. Follow through on your policy. College policies range from non-acceptance to total acceptance.

> One of my colleges has a no cell phones policy in classrooms. I supported and enforced this policy. I reviewed the policy with students on the first day of class and "confiscated" cell phones when they appeared. This policy was specific to this college and student body– vocational/younger students/highly structured courses.

> Another college did not have a policy and had a different student body – older students/less structured classes. At this college, I allowed student cell phone use but I incorporated cell phones into in-class group activities. I asked students to find information online using their cell phones or computers. This way, I could direct students to more appropriate websites and comment on their web research.

Think about your college policy regarding cell phones. If you do not want cell phones in class, then verify what you can "do" to students. Can you throw them out of class? Mark their participation grade down? Or do nothing and if the student fails, then that is his/her responsibility?

ONLINE CLASSES

Classes in the online format have particular issues not common to the on-campus classroom. Online classes require students to be self-motivated in participation, research, and writing. While many students believe that online is somehow less rigorous or less academic, this is not valid. Online classes require more focused effort from students and a higher caliber of research and writing. Nevertheless, students sometimes enroll in online hoping to squeeze in a few quick minutes of online messaging that they believe suffices as a discussion. As instructors, you know that concise, well organized, and well researched posts and papers are necessary for valid learning.

1. Practice netiquette in postings. Netiquette is internet (or network) etiquette. Be clear about your grammar and spelling requirements for online emails and postings. Include a list of netiquette rules, or a link to online netiquette rules.

> The same rules apply in all electronic formats, right? No! With the proliferation of texting and quick email as communicating, some students think that the same format can be used in online classes. Abbreviations are common, vowels are missing, and spellcheck is absent.

> Your postings and emails are the role model for your students. Use proper grammar, punctuation, and

spelling. Do not write in all lower case – this makes the sender seem unaware of grammar and spelling rules. Do not shout (no all capitals) and be polite. Write in complete sentences. Use student names and sign your emails and posts.

My emails include my signature with title and degrees, college name, college website, and phone number (if appropriate). This can be done in almost all email programs, including college emails.

When sending emails, I include the student's name or if a class email, I write " Hello History 122 Class!" I do the same when posting online to an individual student or to the class. I sign my posts. This is also lets students know how they can address you in communications. For example: Prof. M., Ms. Macek, or Jo.

2. Meet and exceed the institution minimum instructor posting requirement. Most institutions have a minimum requirement for instructor posts to the class each week. Do more than is expected; your students and your college will appreciate your interaction.

Your college might require posting/responding 4 of 7 days or to 25% of student posts in each discussion forum. If this is the case, post 5 out of 7 days or to

30% of student posts. By posting regularly, you are showing your students (and administrators) that you are on top of the class and in tune with students.

If you are an overachiever, try for 90% or more student response and daily posts. This is not that difficult. If you have 35 students in a class, you can respond to 5 or 6 students each day and still have a day off from posting.

My goals are to reply to 100% of students in each discussion forum each week. I reply to a few initial student posts each day and can also reply to subsequent student replies throughout the week. In my student evaluations, students often state that I am the most active instructor they have had. And, if you have ever taken an online class in which the instructor almost never responded to your postings, you know that the comment from an instructor to your post is valuable to your learning.

3. <u>Read and answer student questions daily</u>. The questions might be posted to the course or in your email. The online timetable is different than the standard college course meeting week. Most online classes require submission of homework at the end of the week – usually Saturday or Sunday.

Students usually begin these assignments a few days before – Friday evening or Saturday. If Sunday is the deadline, you will receive questions about the homework Saturday day and Sunday day. Answering homework questions in a timely manner is key for student satisfaction and good homework assignments. This does not mean that students procrastinate (even though they do) or that students are not proactive in assignments (which they often are not) but that sometimes students have last minute formatting or reference or content questions.

During the week-end, I check my email twice daily, in the morning and evening.

4.   <u>Resolve online issues immediately.</u> A student might write something without thinking – then post the comment to the class. This might be an offending remark, a bad joke, or a swear word.

Check your university's policy about such postings. This is important - follow policy. Delete the post or ask tech support to delete the post after you copy the post. Contact the student regarding the post and explain why the post was inappropriate. Some institutions require notification to the dean or some such department of inappropriate posts.

Sometimes students become combative in an online environment. This is probably not something she/he would do in an on campus class. If the posts are nasty (swear words, insulting), follow your college's policies. I delete these posts and communicate with the students individually by email or phone.

For example: "Susan, I deleted your post of 01/01/2010 in the World History Discussion week 5 due to the use of swear words – expletives (bad words) throughout the post. Please review the University policy on page 20 of the catalog regarding this policy. If you have further questions or comments, you can email me or the Dean at (123) 456-7890. A University is a place to exchange ideas and information, but we must be respectful of others in the class."

Most of the time, students acknowledge their errors in the use of inappropriate words in the class and are apologetic. In my experience, while I deleted a few posts I have never had a student express anger or belligerence. However, if this happens, contact your department chair.

Save these posts in a file for that student. If there is a question about the reason for the deletion or grade, you will have supporting information.

5.   Establish your online personality.   Our personalities come through online just as they do on campus. In online, however, students only get a small glimpse of instructors rather than a weekly three hour lecture. You can be funny or academic but choose your words carefully. We know that 80% of communication is body language and voice tone in any lecture or presentation. In the online environment, words are the only method to relay information. Make sure your students know you are joking or are emphasizing a point.

In my postings I sometimes use text terms – "LOL". I also use "Yipes!" or emoticons: ☺ or ☹ . Make sure you are clear on your context. This is not the time to exhibit subtle message or sarcasm. Most students, even if older adults, do not understand or appreciate sarcasm or subtly in an online post from an instructor who will be grading them. You might include personal examples (stories) or others' examples of situations that illuminate the topic.

Example: "Gee, Bob, this is interesting. ☺ I like this example of management techniques." (you can go on to include another example or to support with a theory or information from the text.

Academic posts – ones in which large, multiple syllable words are used – are okay, but I suggest explaining these words. I do not "dumb down" posts. I have my personal style of communication, yet I understand that not all students understand all vocabulary words. I might include the definition of an unusual word in parenthesis or include an example.

6. <u>Think and wait before you post or send an email</u>. A student might write something with which you disagree, or that is just plain wrong or dumb. You might be tempted to immediately respond with your opinion or a sarcastic remark. Do not do this!

Email magnifies and distorts the importance of words; students will misinterpret your words to be insulting or derogatory. If you must, write an email or post as a word processing document then wait several hours before you send it. Then do not send the email or post! More times than not, a student – or instructor – is emotional about a topic or other student's post and wants to express his or her opinions (*feelings*). While this may be okay to the Facebook social media community, the classroom is not appropriate to vent non-professional academic setting.

Focus on an appropriate and correct response to the student. Think about a correction to a student's mistaken comment or angry remark rather than lashing at the student.

Example: "Susan, I understand that you are anti-gun control by your comments. However, think about the validity of these sources. In this critical thinking class, think about the source of the information, author, etc. This is discussed in chapter 3. Please make sure that you include relevant, statistically supported information."

7.   <u>Resist the temptation to become a technology teacher (unless that is your subject area).</u>   Students have a wide range of technology experience in online classes or hybrid classes (combination of on campus and online).

If a student is totally lost in the navigation of the online platform, suggest that the student contact technical support. Because you are the instructor, students expect <u>you</u> to have the answers for everything associated with the course and that includes <u>their</u> computer and any software programs they have. You will get bogged down if you are trying to teach students how to attach or convert a document. You need your time to teach course content.

Even in classes taught in an online format, students come with various degrees of computer knowledge.

I have had students who did not know how to:

Save a document in Word

Attach a document

Save a document in richtext

Save to a drive (USB or other)

Compose a PowerPoint (or what a PowerPoint is)

Upload a document

This might also be a great opportunity to refer students to YouTube videos or Jing. I have a few Jing (recorded screen videos) about simple computer techniques(as well as a few subject matter presentations). Do you want to be responsible for the deletion or crashing of a student's computer? Of course not. Do you want to spend an hour or two talking to a student to explain the specifics of saving in Word rather than notepad? Of course not. Most colleges have IT (technology) departments to assist students.

Of course, the same is valid for you. Just because a friend of a friend recommended computer patch does not mean this will work for you.

8. <u>Think about what you want your students to learn in the online discussion threads.</u> Online discussions are very different than on-campus discussions. On campus, the instructor asks a question and usually 3, 4, or 7 students reply. A discussion of a few or several minutes occurs. The instructor's initial question leads to other questions and responses, hence the 'discussion'. In an on-campus discussion, most of the students do not respond to the initial instructor question.

In online classes, all students respond to the same posted question. Open ended questions are important. You must craft discussion questions to elicit a variety of answers, not the same answer posted by 30 different students.

Example #1: What influence did Roman politics have on family life?
This is a recall question and students can only respond with information about Roman family life. Students will not discuss colonization, art, expansion, emperors, military, and so on. This question is limited regarding responses. This would be a good on-campus question because this can lead

to other aspects of Roman politics because on-campus questioning is limited as to the number of students who respond and the time frame of response.

Example #2: Identify a work of art or literature that represents romanticism, realism, or impressionism. Select a work that has not already been used by another student in this discussion. Explain or summarize the work, identify the school of art with which it is associated, and discuss the political, religious, or social influences from the period. When possible, provide a link to a Web page with an image or copy of the artist's work.

In this online question students must research and explain their choice which can be expanded upon by you and other students.

9. <u>Pre-write your posts/replies to students</u>. Some institutions have pre-set discussion questions. Students answer these questions and instructors reply to these student posts. After responding to a few students, you might be tempted to reply "I agree" to the next 20 or so posts. Research and write a set of replies/posts that addresses the discussion for the week. This may include information from the textbook or readings, a scenario, case study, suggested weblink/YouTube video, or other interesting tidbit of information.

Will this seem canned to students? No, because what you write will conform to the discussion question or the topic discussed that week. The key with this method is to copy/paste the pertinent part of the student's comment, then add your own reply.

Example:

My pre-written/post reply: Ethnocentrism is judging other cultures based upon our own. We have certain values and belief systems which we think are correct. We have very valid (rational) reasons for doing what we do in our culture, so of course we think we are 'right'. However, often this is true of other culture or other people. They think their culture is right and other cultures are wrong. When we look for universals – commonalities in all cultures – we can understand and explore why certain cultures do what they do.

Susie Student post: Culture includes visible tangible good, collections of myths and ideas, and also the underlying belief systems not apparent to the eyes. Differences in such tangible goods as food, clothing, and dance are readily apparent. We can often identify the other culture with these tangible goods. Sometimes we question whether other cultures share any of our own cultural attributes.

My reply to Susie Student:

"Susie stated: Sometimes we question whether other cultures share any of our own cultural attributes.

JMacek reply: Ethnocentrism is judging other cultures based upon our own. We have certain values and belief systems which we think are correct. When we look for universals – commonalities in all cultures – we can understand and explore why certain cultures do what they do."

Please note that I referenced part of Susie's post and added my own information, part of which was from my pre-written post.

10. <u>One of your posts to students should be</u>: a web link, academic book recommendation, relevant movie recommendation (a documentary for example), museum recommendation, event recommendation, professional organization recommendation, or site recommendation.

You should state why this is a good book and provide a brief review. When you recommend a book (academic) that is used in your field, you are showing your knowledge and reinforcing your qualifications to teach the course. Chances are that most students will never read that book, see the movie, or join the organization. On the other hand, one of your students might find time between classes to read one of your recommendations. This could be a great learning experience.

Example: A great book about this time period is Jared Diamond's *Guns, Germs, and Steel* that received the Pulitzer Prize in 1998. Professor Diamond wrote about all of the questions we have today about why certain societies had great accomplishments while others did not. What is important to understand, according to Professor Diamond, are the available resources. Not all societies had the same resources – animals, plants, etc.

11. <u>Your postings would be written as short, brief paragraphs with lots of white space.</u> Long, dissertation type messages are too cumbersome, too long, and too straining on the eyes. Even as professionals, we do not read the page long memos sent to us from our institution. Students also rarely read the long, block-style posts or lectures.

Most textbooks today break printing by including graphs, photographs, text-boxes with case studies, or quotes. You should do the same. It is better to write two shorter messages or paragraphs that students will read, than one big long message that students probably will not.

Example: Payment for labor is part of a large complex system. Tangible goods are not exchanged; labor is purchased.

An object has a specific worth and is useful to the owner. Labor, however, is changeable in worth.

A bowl is a useful object. A bowl can hold soup or fruit. A bowl can be packed and taken away, given to another person, left to the grandkids in a will. It has value by the fact that it is an object.

Labor, on the other hand, is intangible. Labor can be paid per hour, per week, or per piece.

One person can earn X dollars for one hour of labor, while another person can earn five times that amount for the same labor.

If a laborer is injured and cannot work, the labor (work performed by the laborer) does not exist and therefore does not have value.

12. <u>Use appropriate in-text citations and reference format in your postings.</u> Provide your students with examples of proper in-text citations or references. If you expect your students to post in APA or MLA format, then you should also. You are the role model students can follow.

> Example: According to Sanday (1981), "In animal economies where hunting or animal husbandry constitutes the main subsistence focus, women do more work than men" (p. 81).

> Sanday, P. (1981). *Female power and male dominance: On the origins of sexual inequality.* New York: Cambridge University Press.

13. <u>Do not answer every student post with another question.</u> If student postings answer the question adequately, adding your own information provides the student with additional insight. On the other hand, if the student post lacks information, ask the student to explain or direct the student otherwise. If you ask the student a question, the student will respond, then you must respond to the student's response. This could go on forever.   Positive feedback tells the student his/her post is complete.

> Example #1:   David, this is excellent information about the causes of the Great War.   Serbian

independence was an important factor.

Example #2: David, please expand on the Black Hand. Who are they and what did they do? Why was this group important to the beginning of the Great War?

14. <u>Your replies to student posts should be more than "good job" or "I agree".</u> Neither of these brief statements provides the student with any meaningful information. If you agree, then state why and provide examples and references.

> Example: Susan, your points about cultural characteristics are excellent. Sociologist Robin M. Williams listed the core values of American culture. These include: individualism, achievement and success, science, and freedom.

15. <u>Read all of a student's post.</u> You might be tempted to skim student posts and replies. I urge you to read all of every post. You might come across inappropriate words, inaccuracies of information, inappropriately expressed ideas, or a great potential learning experience. Reading all posts gives you the opportunity to address concerns or correct any misinformation immediately. Remember that other students will see this post, possibly before you.

You should:

Correct information before other students think this
to be fact

Delete "bad" language (see your college policy about
    this)

Delete or correct assignment misconceptions/
    inaccuracies

Correct or respond to lax responses (because
    students think a one sentence post or reply is okay
    if you do not say anything)

Posts to the incorrect discussion forum

16. Respond to specific student posts. Comment on student
comments, ask probing questions, and guide students in their
research and exploration of material. When you reply to a student,
use his/her name and address specific information in his/her post.
When you reply to a student post, you are using the traditional
Socratic question-answer method that allows the student to gain
insight.

> Example: Susan, you have an interesting comment
> about capitalism and globalization. US businesses
> must sell their goods somewhere, one place is in
> underdeveloped and/or poor nations. Our own
> economy benefits from these sales. Why should we
> "care" if people from poorer nations buy these
> products? Keep going with your ideas on this.

17. <u>Be present in your class.</u> Being present does not mean sitting at your computer 24/7. Being present means spacing postings throughout the week, sending class or individual emails when appropriate, and posting announcements weekly or twice each week.

> When students know you are reading their comments and accessing the class regularly, they are more likely to respond to your posts and announcements. I reply to about 5 students each day throughout the week. For a class of 25 or 30, this means I will have replied to everyone during the week. And I also can comment to replies of my replies.
>
> Send a weekly welcome or announcement at the beginning of each week. I post and send to students, an overview of the week one or two days before the beginning of the week.   I also post a general announcement during the week.

18. <u>Accept student comments.</u> Never in your wildest imaginations would you believe that students reach certain conclusions or post outlandish ideas; yet this happens. Do not ridicule the student. Correct the misinformation, if appropriate, and supply an alternative/correct idea.

> Example:

Christopher College post: When we entered into World War II, like when we did, we lead the way. The power nations, Great Britain and France, sat by while this happened and did not react, or attempt to, until their territory was threatened.

JMacek reply: A correction is needed here, Christopher. The US entered WWII in 1941 when Japan attacked Pearl Harbor in December 7. A few days later, Germany declared war on the US and the US responded and began fighting in Europe.

Please note that Great Britain and France had been fighting Germany since 1939, several years before the US entered WWII. More information is in your text on pages 250 to 253.

19. Students do not know how to spell. Do not ridicule the student. You might send a personal email about correct spelling. Then, submit your own post with the correct spelling.

Students write about "Marx and *Lennon*" or about the "violent society that we live in with theft, carjacking, and *cereal* killers." These are real posts from real students!

Example: My reply: "Christopher College, yes, Karl Marx and Vladimir Lenin greatly influenced the formation of communist Russia."

20.   Students have poor grammar skills in online classes.   Often, students do not capitalize proper nouns, use the wrong tense, or ignore punctuation rules.   This may be because they believe that spelling and grammar do not matter in online classes.   Sometimes they post from cell phones that require additional time or key strokes for composing proper comments.

> If you accept (give full credit) grammar and spelling errors, then students believe this behavior is acceptable and will continue with bad grammar and bad spelling. Do not ignore bad grammar and bad spelling.
>
> Think about sending a general email at the beginning of the course about the importance of proper spelling and grammar and that spelling and grammar are part of posting grades. This may be (possibly should be) part of your grading rubric. Yes, I know, you included this in your syllabus. However, the syllabus is crammed with policy information and sometimes these very important details get lost in the reams of paper.
>
> If a student posts an egregiously bad comment, I send a personal email to the student about the post. If the post is too horrid (swearing, insulting, etc), I

delete the post and email the student. Some colleges have policies regarding insulting posts. Check the policy of your college.

In grading, I inform students that the reason they did not receive full credit was due to spelling and grammar errors.

Example #1: A good post. But watch spelling and grammar – this brought your grade down.

Example #2: Susie, you have good information in your post but please watch your grammar and spelling. There are too many spelling errors in this post.

Example #3: Christopher, while your information was good, the spelling in your post detracted from your message. The grading rubric for discussion posts states that 1 point will be deducted for spelling errors. Please note the following errors are underlined in your post: "Even though Charlemagne was barely literate that he was a very intellugent man, I was surprised that he was intelligent nit being abke to read well. The fact that he was able to rule his kingdom successfully with such limited education was inspiring to me and made me have a certain respect for him."

21. <u>Most students want to do the right thing online</u>. You may read some of these examples of student writing and think that (1) today's students are doomed forever to be working in the fast food industry, or (2) I am absolutely making this up, or (3) students will be "ticked-off" if you correct them, or (4) your job does not entail correcting minor grammar and spelling errors and students should know this already.

> None of the above is valid. Depending upon the student demographics of your college, the students may have exceptional writing skills so you will not need to remind them of checking spelling and such, or your student are in an open enrollment institution that accepts almost everyone and your student absolutely must be reminded of spelling and grammar issues. These students need to understand the importance of written communication in the professional setting. Your primary job may be to teach psychology or marketing or biology subject matter but your secondary job is to also teach students to be professionals.

> Most students will acknowledge their errors and many will apologize. Students want to learn – this

is why they are in college. They might state that they sent the message late in the day and they were tired but wanted to get a post before the deadline. Or, they may not know the correct spelling for that word (especially a technical or industry specific term). Or, their minds were faster than their fingers can type – I call this the *"fast finger syndrome."* A person is so focused on writing the message that she/he forgets the spelling and grammar.

A note: We have all suffered from incorrect grammar and spelling. (Please do not get me started on the use of "they" when referring to a singular person! And this is from people with advanced degrees!)

22.   <u>Include your personal experiences.</u> Students who enroll in online courses are often also working or have other time constraints that prohibit them from enrolling in on-campus classes. Working students need to reaffirm that the material they are learning is applicable to their career aspirations. Include examples of applications of the information presented in class. You might also ask students to include their experiences.

I posted this to an online history class: Many years ago I taught high school in a very diverse school near Detroit, Michigan. The student body was

African-Americans, immigrant Bosnians, Croatians, and Serbs (Eastern Europe); white American; Hispanic, and a few Asian-Americans in addition to "white" (European) Americans.

Being knowledgeable about the history of these cultures and how each responds to authority figures (me) was very helpful in quelling classroom issues. For example, I knew that two students from Bosnia were from different towns that had a history of hostility towards each other. I physically separated these students in the classroom, seating them at opposite ends of the class.

23. <u>Use real world experiences to illustrate theoretical points.</u> Incorporate information from recent news headlines. This shows students that you can relate to them and students can readily relate to information to which they have access. They can investigate themselves and sometimes do so. This may be a great learning and research opportunity for students.

Example: One argument against anthropologists in the military is that researchers are not prepared or trained as military personnel and cannot protect themselves in dangerous situations. In 2008, two researchers were killed while working for the military in the US conflict in Iraq and Afghanistan.

This is a link to the news article: XXXXXX

What do you think about this?

24. Use Bloom's taxonomy in developing discussion questions. Bloom's taxonomy is a hierarchical evaluative rubric. If you are not familiar with Bloom's taxonomy and want to teach, then you absolutely must research this.

> Bloom's taxonomy classifies thinking/knowledge into different levels from the simplest level of recall of facts to the most complex levels of evaluating and creating. To recall information is to memorize and recite. To evaluate or create is to make decisions about arguments with supporting information and to design or develop new views or ideas. (Research this. Bloom's taxonomy is important on many levels.)

> Simple recall information – remembering what the book or lecture said – is the lowest step in Bloom's taxonomy. Recall questions in an online format will give you 30 of the same answers – in other words, all of the students will restate the material presented. If you want recall, that is fine; on the other hand, if you want students to analyze, synthesize or evaluate material, then you should develop these types of questions. You might use

recall for quizzes or homework.

Example #1: Q: In English, there are many terms for the word "money". How many terms for money can you think of, and what are their different meanings?

This is really a recall question. This question is not asking for evaluation or synthesis or a variety of examples. Even though this is asking for the students' interpretations, the answers are finite and you will get repetitive answers. Also, think of how you would respond to these posts.

Examples #2: Q: Using the chapters as a foundation to understanding politics and conflict, review two Internet sites on a conflict of your choice from 1900 to present. Discuss the situation reflecting on causation, role of social stratification, type of conflict (revolution, civil war, feud), and the resolution or results of the conflict. Respond to at least two other students' postings.

This question requires synthesis and evaluation of the material discussed in the chapters. This question is designed to make sure the student understands these particular theories and definitions, to provide an example, and to substantiate this example.

25. <u>Include a separate introduction forum so student can say hello to each other.</u>   Include a forum so students can introduce themselves and start to become a community and builds communication among students. This should be the first, or one of the first, discussion boards which students should post.

Provide guidelines for introductions. This might include name, major, career goals, interesting fact about themselves, what they want to gain from the class, an amusing anecdote, etc. Students should be required to respond to one or more other students. This should be a graded post, or students will not respond.

Respond to each student. Do not just state "hello" or "welcome to class". Include a line asking about the student, an encouraging word, or other note; show that you are interest in each student.

I have a pre-written post that I copy/paste and adjust accordingly. This way, I can recognize the student and comment about something specific in their post. Make your reply to the student personal by including his/her name.

26. <u>Send a welcome email to students before the beginning of the class.</u> This shows students you are looking forward to the class, and is also a reminder for students who forgot they registered. Include the class name, beginning date, and your contact information. I send an email to students a few days before the beginning of the class and I also post as an announcement to the class. If your college allows late (after start date) admissions to classes, send a welcome note to these students also. This will make them feel welcome and part of the class.

Example: Hello Students in Anthropology 100!
Please share your thoughts and viewpoints in the various discussion forums throughout the course.

The major, major, major (yes, that's 3 majors!) issue in anthropology is being open to the ideas of "the other". I place the other in quotation marks because that is how cultures often view the people of other cultures - as "others" or outsiders.

In studying other cultures, we should be open to differences values, behaviors, and ways of thinking. This is a challenge. Are you up for it? Do you think you have an open mind?

I look forward to the beginning of class on Monday, September 4. If you have questions, please email me at jtmacek@xyzcollege.edu.

I look forward to discussing anthropology issues with you in the coming weeks.

> Jo Macek, MAT
> XYZ College
> jtmacek@xyzcollege.edu

27. .Expect tangent discussions. A tangent discussion can be a teachable moment or chaos. Student conversations will swerve from the discussion topic and go in any direction imaginable. This is just like a live campus discussion.

> If the discussion is beneficial to the class and new knowledge is shared then continuing the discussion may be a teachable moment. You might add additional information (references, weblinks, etc). You might also post information to the class via "announcement page" or class email telling students to check out a particular discussion thread. However, do not overuse announcements or emails. If students receive too many of these emails, they will only glance at these or just delete them.

Example: "Hello History 250 Students. Check out discussion forum #2 for this week. Even though we are discussing WWI, Oliver Online posted some great information about the Battle of Stalingrad in WWII. Pictures and great links!"

Sometimes students start a discussion that is covered later in the class. In this case, ask students to keep a note of their ideas and post to the future discussion forum, or you might do the same. Make a copy or note of these comments, then highlight these in the appropriate discussion.

Example: "Susie, This information is great! You have some great information regarding technology marketing techniques and globalization. We will be discussing the technology companies in depth in week 4. How about holding on to these ideas and re-posting this information to discussion #1 during week 4? I know others will appreciate this information, and can also add additional information."

If the discussion is not worthwhile, corral the students and divert them back to the original topic.

Example: "Susie and Oliver, This is an interesting discussion about organizational behavior of manufacturing companies. However, please remember that we are discussing market trends and economics this week. You might continue this discussion in the "café" section of class. Information sharing is good. ☺"

28. <u>Discussion posts should have deadlines sometime mid-week.</u> If posts are due at the end of the week, then the majority of students will post on the due date.

> If the deadline is Sunday, this means that the 20 or 30 students will post (and reply) on Saturday or Sunday. Students will have minimal interaction with each other and with you. If initial posts are due mid-week (perhaps Wednesday or Thursday) then replies by the end of the week, this will give you the opportunity to respond to students throughout the remainder of the week. Students posting on Friday or Saturday can reply to your replies.

> Are you confused yet? Basically, if you tell a person (student or not) that something is due on Friday, then you will receive that thing on Friday. This means your response must be on Friday or more probably Saturday. This does not give you or your students enough time to access others' posts

and "digest" or research the information.

29. <u>Log in the day discussion posts are due.</u> Logging in later in the day is better as most of the students will have posted. This is your best time to respond to students and also gives students the opportunity to respond to you later in the week. This gets a discussion going.

30. <u>Motivate your students.</u>   The beginning of class always generates excitement. However, by the middle or end of class, students drop when they realize they have commitments, etc. Keep your students motivated to keep reading the book, researching materials, and posting to the discussions forums.

> Motivation is more than stating "keep going" or "good work".   Motivation should include questioning, "what if" questions, personal experiences, or humor can encourage students. If a student has not posted in a week or so (or whatever your college requirements might be), send the student an email.
>
> Example #1: Christopher, This was a good post but keep going! You have some great ideas here about integrating marketing techniques into social media. How about some specific examples?

Example #2: Oliver, We are in week 5 but I show that you did not respond to the discussion posts in week 4. Are you still interested in completing the class? Please contact me as soon as possible.

Example #3: Hello Class! Attached is an interesting YouTube video about using social media in marketing. Have you had experience as a consumer or producer of this type of media? What do you think (good/bad/indifferent)? There might be issues about confidentiality and your personal information with regards to this. What are your thoughts?

31. <u>Being academic is okay, but be aware of the level of your students.</u> Freshmen are still learning theory, concepts, and terminology. They may not understand your references to particular researchers or the nuances of terminology. Likewise, colleges have different student demographics that have diverse educational backgrounds.

Vocabulary should be clear and straightforward. This applies to your everyday words that students might not know. If you think students might not understand certain words, include a synonym in parentheses or use a different word. You might be tempted to say here that students should learn more vocabulary words.   While I agree with expanding one's vocabulary, the excellent student will find the word in a dictionary, the average (or less than) student will not and will not understand your comments. A synonym or explanation will not insult the excellent student and will help the average (or less than average) student.

If you refer to certain researchers or books/articles/etc, also include the reason for your inclusion.

32. <u>Tackling synchronous discussions</u>. Synchronous means 'real-time'. This would be a real-time discussion with your student or groups of students.

Real-time can be cumbersome because students live in different time zones (and that is just the US). If your college has set times, then your students should be aware of these set times for meeting online.   On the other hand, if a synchronous meeting (or two or more) is required but the instructor is responsible for setting these, then pre-planning is important.

In the pre-class welcome, send a note about any required live meetings.   This gives students the opportunity to change classes if they cannot meet in a real-time environment. Lest you think these students are lax, remember that not all students have the required technology to communicate in real-time or the student might be an international student living in India who cannot meet at 2AM your time and who has limited internet capabilities. (This is real concern.)

If the synchronous meeting is required once or twice during the term, then I suggest offering a few available times. Give your students three or four times when you can meet with the group or class then ask students to choose a time. Do not ask our students when they are available. This is much too cumbersome to try to coordinate around the schedule of 30 or so students. Set a specific time limit (1 hour, 2 hours) for the discussion depending upon the discussion format and goals.

Technology glitches abound. Test your equipment days prior to the meeting and ask students to check theirs. Include a technology help number in your emails so students can fix any tech problems prior to the synchronous meeting. Test software and microphones.

Provide students with the agenda prior to the meeting. Provide questions to students before the meeting time. Just as in on campus classes, students will remain quiet if surprised with questions, and will wait for someone to say something. This means that the instructor or one or two students will monopolize the discussion.

If you do not provide an agenda or questions prior to the meeting, you will get dead air time. Dead air in synchronous meetings is a curse on the class; time is amplified when sitting at a computer without noise. This is much worse in online synchronous live meetings with active voice discussions if no one says anything. An agenda will provide students with the information to be discussed and a Q/A sheet will tell students what you plan to ask about their projects or research so they are not cause off-guard and answer "duh" in front of their classmates. (Listen to a talk radio program and you will find that the announcer never has any dead air time s/he is always saying something to keep you (the listener) interested.)

The only silence should be at the end of the discussion when everyone leaves the connection. I end the session but tell students I will remain connected if anyone has a question or wants to chat about the material.

Get students involved in synchronous discussions by dividing them into groups or asking questions. Depending upon the technology, you can divide students into groups to discuss questions then to bring their ideas to the whole class. Adobe Connect, for example, does this. Do not let students have too much time in this group or they will become distracted by their home environments. Remember that you are competing with children, spouse, dogs/cats/hamsters, laundry, dinner/lunch/ breakfast, and whatever else is due that day. Make all students say something during the synchronous class.

33. <u>Summarizing weekly discussions.</u> Some colleges require a weekly summary (what we discussed and learned this week. If the summary is an announcement at the end of the week, then students will probably not review this because the information pertained to last week.). If you post this then send this as an email so students will read the information.

34. <u>Timing discussion posts.</u> Some instructors/colleges allow access to discussion questions for duration of the course and allow

students to post early. This means that some students might post two or more weeks in advance. Some allow students to view the questions (in a syllabus), but lock out the discussions to prohibit early posting. Others reveal questions on weekly and have deadlines for postings. There are advantages and disadvantages to each method.

Student to can post early to all discussions might do so thereby not gaining the important information from your weekly lectures/guidance or possibly of the interaction during the week. On the other hand, these students might have time commitments (military or travel, for example) that would preclude them from posting during a set time frame. After all, this is why the student is enrolled in an online not on campus class.

Seeing the discussion question before the deadline post allows the student to research and write the reply before the assignment due date. However, if you are the instructor who sometimes changes assignments/due dates/questions, then students will have gathered the information only to have the requirement changed at the last minute then do more research and work for something due that week. This can be very frustrating for students who plan assignments.

Revealing discussion questions and homework assignments on a weekly basis ensures that students focus on these questions and assignments. On the other hand, this limits the time students can research the information for an assignment or question to less than one week. We know as degreed faculty that researching credible information – even in today's internet availability – takes time and patience.

Closing a discussion forum prevents students from posting. However, students who have technology difficulties or other time constraints (travel, health, military) may not be able to post by the deadline date. Yes, his/her post would be late.

I know some of my students have had dealt with storms that interrupted their internet (and other utilities) or other disasters. One of my students contacted me the day after a post was due to inform me that his house and all of the contents burned to the ground a few days ago. He attached his post to the email hoping I would accept it.

Some colleges might have policies regarding late assignments so you cannot accept late work. Be aware of these policies. Also, some colleges require a minimum number of days that students post during the week. If students post early or if you keep the discussion open, students may not meet the minimum college requirements. Know the policy of your college.

35. Use specific participation criterion/rubric for postings. What exactly is an "A" grade post? You might say this includes examples, synthesis of information, evaluation, spelling/grammar, etc. Provide an example of an A post as well as a failing (E) post. Include a minimum word count and how much can be quotes. This may seem trivial, but students cannot read your mind to assess your specific requirements for postings and students come from various educational backgrounds. Stating a post must be "substantive" or "clear" or "provide examples" is not giving too much information to students. If you believe an excellent post to a discussion question should require at least 250 words not including one 20 to 30 word quote plus two references, then state this. Otherwise students will not know to include this information. If you want students to write in a block essay or Q/A format, then advise them.

Example #1:

Postings should be insightful, thorough, interesting. Insightful posting is one that discusses the question with clear and deep perception. It will displays good deductive reasoning, which is a conclusion, made by the poster, related to the topic that is supported by evidence especially concepts from the readings.

Thorough posting is one that is painstakingly accurate or careful in its discussion of the question. It will completely answer all parts of the question.

Interesting posting is one that is related to the topic and holds the attention of the reader. It will relate concepts in a way different from the readings and make them more relevant to the question discussed.

Example #2:

Initial posting answering the discussion question should be at least 250 words. Initial posts and replies should include references in APA format (references and quotes are NOT included in word count). Replies should add to the general knowledge of the class. Merely stating agreement or restating post will not earn credit. Replies should be at least 150 words.

Student posting and responses will be assessed according to the following criteria:

Clarity: Focus on a specific topic and context, provide examples, avoid vague generalities.

Accuracy: Give correct information that others can verify.

Precision: Provide specific details that support all comments.

Relevance: Connect to the issues currently.

Depth and breadth: Address the problem from many points of view; consider how others might

Significance: Focus on the most important elements of a topic or elements that others have overlooked; avoid repeating common knowledge.

Example #3:

What do you think of this post? Would you give this student and "A"? I did. Please note word count and referencing in APA format. Please note the specific statistics provided and evaluation and conclusion provided by the student.

According to Carson (2010), at European contact in 1500, about 5,000 indigenous groups existed in the "new world" of South America. Today, only 400 groups exist in South America. Within about 150 years after initial contact, about 50 million people died. Many died from European diseases, either deliberately or accidentally introduced to the Americas. Other changes that affected indigenous peoples were the forced European style systems of farming and European plants; this was a drastic change in diet and eating habits.

Today, about 11% of the people in Latin America are indigenous. The largest groups are in Peru, Mexico, Guatemala, Bolivia, and Ecuador.

About 90% are subsistence farmers. The life expectancy is 10-20 years less than average, partly due to less accessibility to education and health care. Gender is also a factor; for example, a non-indigenous man earns 14 times more than an indigenous woman (Carson, 2011).

After contact in the 1500s, the Spanish became the 'gente decente' who were civilized, urban, Roman Catholic, and governing class. The early Spanish settlers killed indigenous peoples who did not kneel to the Spanish government. However, the Spanish spoke in the Spanish language, not in the language of the tribe. Thousands were killed because they did not understand what they should do.

The indigenous peoples continued to be marginalized by economic development, class, gender, and social relations. Throughout history, various governments and individuals took advantage of indigenous peoples. In parts of Central and South America, paramilitary forces burned villages and killed thousands to clear land.

Carson, G. (2020). Modern Latin America. New
York: Random House.

36.   <u>Add a discussion boards for questions about the syllabus
(assignments).</u>   Number the pages of your syllabus so you and
students can locate information.   You can even copy and paste
from the syllabus and explain further.   One specific forum will
keep other discussion boards free for discussions.

37.   <u>Lecture/lesson/guidance posts.</u>   Some institutions require a
weekly lecture or lesson or guidance or instruction for the week.
This is usually an overview of the assignments, focuses student
readings, and provides an explanation of the material if needed.   If
you teach the same course several times, you can pre-write these
lessons. However, keep up with any textbook, assignment, or
discussion question changes.   You can post these within the
weekly folders, possibly as an announcement, or as a weekly email
to students.   Lessons might not always be written.   Would a
presentation, your YouTube video, or audio presentation suffice as
your weekly lesson?

38.   <u>Keep in contact with your students.</u> If a student has not posted
or submitted work in a week (or whatever requirements you set),
send the student an email.   You also want to be aware of your
college's policies about student contact.   Some colleges require
you to submit weekly progress reports.   Be proactive with absent
students, this might prevent a bad situation from getting worse or

you might be able to resolve the issue. At least you will be aware of the situation. A student may have medical issues or technology issues or personal issues. The student may ask for an extension of an assignment, or may plan to drop the class. Or the student misunderstood the assignment or due date.

39.   Use student names or nicknames. Online classes can be impersonal. The legal name of a student might not be his/her preferred name. Usually, the student provides his/her preferred name in the introduction discussion forum. Please note this. We know the importance of names - the proper use of one's preferred name is important to establishing a rapport and positive communication between you and your students. You might note the nickname on a spreadsheet or gradesheet or a file.

40.   Feedback for discussion posts is important. Discussion posts are really mini-essays and as such these should be graded as mini-essays with regards to grammar/spelling/factual support/ organization.

> In today's e-world, most communication is through email. When students are "sloppy" in their emails, this translates to sloppy papers and sloppy professional and personal life. You are training your students to become better and more efficient communicators.

ON CAMPUS CLASSES

On-campus classes have been the standard of higher education for centuries. The "sage on stage" scenario is of learned faculty lecturing (talking at) a student body eagerly waiting to absorb esteemed and valuable knowledge. Another scenario is the small classroom with faculty engaging students in an active Socratic discussion.   Yet another scenario is the active interaction of students facilitated by the instructor.   All of these scenarios are valid in today's college.   Whatever your college, think about the philosophy of your college (mission statement), student demographics, and your teaching style. If you are interactive and want to talk to students, this may not be possible at a college that has large 200+ lecture halls.   If you have a great expanse of knowledge to share and want others to listen to you, then perhaps a college with an older and experienced student body may or may not be to your liking.   Finding your "fit" with a college will be beneficial to you and your students.

1. <u>Lectures should inform as well as interest</u>. In the "olden days" before cell phones, WiFi, or internet, instructors had a captive audience with their lectures. Students did not have the distractions of today, nor did students have the availability for other (competing) information from different sources. In the 21st century student have the ability to see in nearly "real time" the events of the real world.   With the convenience of YouTube videos, streaming videos, twitter, Flickr, and more internet programs than I

can count (!) students can see, hear, and get the information you are presenting in your lecture while you are presenting (!).

Reading from yellowed notes may have been commonplace up to the 1990's but in the 2000's students can download your pirated recorded audio and digitally transcribed lecture. In other words, they can read or hear the information whenever/wherever they want.

If attendance at lecture is important to you and your institution, then re-fashion the "lecture" into "inform and enlighten". While today's students (aged 18 to 48+) think they are more aware of the modern world around them, you and I know this is just not true. Youngsters think because they have the internet that they have the evaluative and analytical capabilities to decipher billions of pieces of information. Not so! (Remember that these are also the people who vote for American Idol because they think their vote counts, and believe the Chris and Rhianna break-up is considered a "major US conflict", and agree with the Kardashian's about foreign policy).

If your response to these three examples is "who? what?" then do not fret. Your parents and instructors thought the same about your interest in Bobby

Darrin and Gidget, Bob Marley, and *Saturday Night Live* with Chevy Chase and John Belushi. We may think each generation is different but really we are not. The events are different, but the importance and feelings are the same.

Older students might fall into the "I know this already" category because they are older than the traditional student (and possibly older than you) so think they are more experienced and knowledgeable. Often, however, their experiences lay in the practical day-to-day rather than the theoretical and analytical aspect of course materials. *They know what they do but do not know why.* Your lectures validate their experiences and lend insight into events and motivations. They can often more readily apply your theory to their work life.

The difference between prior generations and today is the tremendous availability of information at one's fingertips. Today's students really do have less attention span than a few generations ago. Students will "tune out" while listening to monotone lectures. In a large institution with a lecture hall of 500 students, student interaction is nearly impossible. However, the use of pictures, videos, audio, or other presentations can enhance and inform students.

Finding appropriate photographs, etc., may take time, but student will better understand your information. Showing a photograph or video will also divide the lecture and allow you a moment to capture your ideas and for students to use all of their senses in understanding the information you presented. In addition, you can augment your lectures with such technology as blogs, webpage (yours or others), and of course, graduate assistants.

2. Discussions in smaller classes. In classes of less than 50, lectures can include videos, PowerPoints, and even group activities. Class interaction is limited but possible. In these smaller classes, an instructor can use discussions to elicit comments from students. Of course, not all students can or will answer questions but the few comments from students will encourage thinking in others and also enliven your lecture.

Discussion questions should have a purpose. Do not ask questions just to ask. Do not ask recall questions unless these lead to evaluative or analytical questions (Bloom's Taxonomy).

Example #1:
Q: Does anyone remember the causes of the Civil War from your readings?

A: The possible answers are "yes" or "no". (okay for keeping students awake)

Example #2:

Q: What were the causes of the Civil War?

A: Students will recall the information from lectures and readings. (okay for the highly motivated)

Example#3:

Q: Why did President Lincoln suspend habeas corpus during the Civil War?

A: Students will provide several reasons, some valid while others not. You can respond to these. This can develop into other legal and constitutional questions.

Example #4:

Q: What political and social advantage did the radical Republicans hope to gain during Reconstruction?

A: Multiple answers are possible. This can also develop into a discussion of different eras of political influence and change as well as social issues.

Small group discussions are possible in smaller lecture classes. Depending upon the size of the class, students can be grouped into 4 or 5 and discuss a question/problem and bring their findings to the class. In a class of 50, this can be by row or "count off" so you will have 10 groups of 5 students.

Time is important here. Limit the time students can discuss the information and the time to relate their conclusions to the class, but this should only take 10 or 15 minutes of class time. Make sure you relate the time frame to students; i.e., 10 minutes to talk, 15 minutes to talk, etc. Make sure students stay on target. In a 60 minute or 90 minute class, the 15 minutes will integrate students into the class and focus their attention on the material. These group discussions are useful for case study analysis, problem solving, or assimilation of viewpoints.

3. Integrating activities. Activities might include in-class or out of class exercises. As with any activities, these should relate to the course objectives and not be busy work. Think about what you want your students to learn from the activity.

This does not mean that repetition and reinforcement should not be part of homework. Repetition is needed to memorize information and is helpful in learning languages, arithmetic, physiology, chemistry, history, and so forth. This is a basic level of learning. For higher level classes – junior or senior – repetition may not be necessary when evaluative and analyzing information is more appropriate. Today, many textbook publishers include worksheets and activities with textbooks. These, however, are one-size-fits-all and may not be appropriate for your college or students. Again, the key is relating the learning outcome to your course objectives. I suggest trying an activity in one class, if that works well then incorporate into future classes

4. <u>In-class activities can illustrate your point to students</u>. When I integrate in-class group discussions or activities, I use a four step "formula".

I begin with a focus on the topic. This might be a video/activity/survey/QA. This prepares students to focus on the topic. I present the information in a lecture (presentation/video/PPT) which is about 20 minutes (with a few open discussion questions within the lecture), then a group activity that illustrates the information in the lecture that is about 15 minutes. The group activity shows me that student understand or do not understand the material I presented. Then students complete an individual assignment that relates to the topic of the week. This might be a paper or worksheet that incorporates the information from this lecture and/or other lectures. In a three hour class, lecture includes my presentations/lectures, discussion questions, perhaps one YouTube video and three class/group activities. This keeps the class at an even pace while maintaining student interest.

What exactly is an in-class activity? In most texts, the questions at the end of the chapter can be used as in-class activities. You can give the same questions to groups in class to gain different perspectives. (This works well in psychology, sociology, and business classes.). Or different questions to each group – this will give students the opportunity to synthesize information from the readings, your lecture, and other students' perspectives. If the text used has an instructor manual with activities then you might use some of those suggested.

Example #1: For a psychology class, I use a worksheet (from an instructor manual) that lists about 30 examples of different types of conditioning. I divide students into groups then ask students to explain 5 of these. (Group #1 is 1-5, Group #2 is 6-10, etc).

Example #2: For a communication class, I provide different scenarios of interpersonal communications (scripts) and ask students to discuss the sender/receiver/etc. Abbott/Costello's "Who's On First" is the best!

Example #3: In a humanities class, I give students a set of photos of 5 or 6 art pieces from different time periods and ask students to place these into chronological order and present to the class.

Also, for a humanities class, I give modeling clay to students and ask them to fashion a *contrapposto* figure. (Of course no one is able to do this, but this illustrates the difficulties of sculpture and techniques required in art.)

An out of class activity is not the same as an in-class activity. In-class in just that: the duration of the class period. An out-of-class activity can be valuable also. Out-of-class activities might be such individual or group activities as psychology experiments (in lab), surveys, group analysis of case studies or interpretation of literature.

Homework assignment including research papers, worksheets, experiments, or other activities supports your information and reinforces the material learned. After all, if students learned everything they need to know by reading or listening, they would not need you – the faculty member. They could just read the book or listen to PBS.

5. <u>Be cognizant of your college demographics.</u> College student demographics differ; an in-class activity that goes over well in once college may be confusing at another. Completing a simple worksheet may be fine for a vocational/technical college but too elementary for a highly selective university. If you are not sure, you can try the activity. If it works – great! If not, then do not use it again. When I try new activities in class that I am not sure will work out, I tell students that this is the first time for this activity then I solicit feedback on the activity.

> Example: Students used a set of wooden building blocks to "build" a critical thinking argument. This was great at one college - they explained the foundational thesis and supporting facts - but fell flat at another. Students at the first college were kinesthetic learners and vocal about their positions. Students at the other college were more analytical and visual.

6. <u>Students have different learning styles.</u> We process and retain information differently – this is someone's learning style. In-class activities are ways you can address different student learning styles. The three basic learning styles are: visual, auditory, and kinesthetic/tactile. Most of us have a preference for one style, but

use all of these in learning material.

Visual people learn best with visual stimulation: videos/ movies/slides, PowerPoints (or other presentations), colors, pictures, graphs. The majority of people in the US are visual learners – about 60%.

Auditory learners need to hear information, lectures are great for auditory learners as are audio recordings, speeches, oral presentations, group interactions (talking), discussions, or listening to performances. About 20% of the population prefers to learn by hearing.

Kinesthetic/tactile learners learn when their entire bodies are engaged in an activity. These are the foot fidgeters, finger tappers, and seat squirmers in class. They need to be physically engaged so group activities, role-play, model-making, writing on the board/flip chart, presentations in which they are actors are helpful for these students.

7. <u>Student cell phones and computers/iPads.</u> Your policy about student cell phones and/or personal computers should be in your syllabus. If you do not want cell phones and/or personal computers in your on-campus class then note this to your students.

This technology is temptingly distracting for students. However, some students use personal computers to take notes – rather than the "old fashioned" paper-pencil method.

> In my smaller on-campus classes, I "use" student cell phones and computers. I organize students into groups then ask students to find information via internet on their cell phones.

> Example: In humanities, I might give students a list of artists or art works to find online. Or in religious studies, research religious holidays. As students work in groups, I can walk around the class and comment on their websites. This is another way I can oversee students and to guide them in their research – to suggest websites or online journals.

> Cell phone use is your prerogative. You can forbid student use of cell phones. Also, as the instructor, you should turn *your* cell phone off or to vibrate, during class time.

8. Graduate assistants are great. These students learned and are continuing to learn the material while also taking on the burden of making sure other less experienced students understand the concepts you present.

Graduate assistants can be motivational, directed, and enlightening. Or they can be dull, uninspired, and ineffective. If you list the characteristics of a good instructor, then you also have the characteristics of a good graduate student. The graduate student is your responsibility not only in the material he/she learns, but also in his/her treatment and advice to new students. Your graduate student is a reflection of you.

9. <u>PowerPoints and other presentations should be brief without too much text but lots of visuals</u>. Too many words will make your presentation slides to cluttered; students will be too busy trying to copy the material in our slide and will not listen to you. Or the words are so small that on one can see.

Pictures evoke imagery more than explanation. A photograph can "show" your students the concept, then explain.

Too many graphics, colors, font sizes, and other snazzy techniques will only distract students. Keep it simple! Heading, a few bullet points, sub-points, and photograph or graphic. Use a dark background with light letters for PowerPoint presentations - this is easier to read.

GRADING/TESTING

Grading papers can be a time consuming task. In addition to papers, grading students for on-campus participation or on-line participation is sometimes required. Students want relevant and precise feedback for the time and effort they put into composing their papers or online discussion posts. This is an important component for students.

Remember when you attended college and eagerly awaited return of your paper. You eagerly read the instructors comments and criticisms noted in red pen. You wondered why the instructor crossed off, edited, or corrected a word. You may have taken these to heart and corrected the next paper you submitted. Or not.

Each paper was a learning experience for you. Students today are no different. They want to learn, correct errors, and succeed in their academic education.

Colleges often provide little guidance about the methodology of grading papers. Some institutions have formal courses or certificates in college teaching but these courses are not required to become a college instructor. Institutions, students, and instructors believe that if we know the material we are qualified to assess participation and papers.

Multiple choice exams (or essay exams) and quizzes can provide feedback for your students and for you. While students think that test grades are all important, we know tests are only a tool for assessment of learning.

1. <u>Devote a set time each week to grading papers</u>. Set aside a few hours each week for grading papers. Mark this on your calendar. Paper grading has a way of creeping up even when you know you must grade papers. Often, grading takes more time than we think.

> You might have two or three grading sessions of a few hours each. Do not overburden yourself by trying to grade all papers in one sitting, your eyes and mind will become too tired to adequately and objectively grade the assignment. You might also want to review each paper before assigning the final grade for the paper. If students submitted papers on Friday, they want their grades next Friday. Set a few hours over the week-end or during the week to grade a few papers. This way you can spend two hours three or so days during the week to grade papers – not all day on a Saturday or Wednesday. This will keep you fresh and alert.

2. <u>Download the gradesheet from the course website or make your own gradesheet.</u> A gradesheet has the final mark for discussions (participations) and papers. For online classes, however, an initial post then replies are usually required. Keep a log or spreadsheet to track student postings. In on campus classes in which participation is required, you can do the same with a physical spreadsheet.

In online classes, as student posts are read, mark the *initial post* column with a grade for the quality of the post. As students reply, mark the 1st reply or 2nd reply columns. This will save time at the end of the week or grading period because you reviewed the posts and replies already. Either an electric or hardcopy spreadsheet is helpful. With a hardcopy, notions are made in long-hand then transferred to the gradesheet. With an electronic version, one window should be open for the spreadsheet and one for the online discussion.

In on campus courses, a hardcopy form can be at the desk or podium then transferred to the gradesheet. This can also provide proof for students who question the rationale for their discussion or participation grade.

You can apply a rubric to participation grading. A rubric is a standard of performance. A rubric is a grid-type measurement in which I include certain participation requirements. For on campus classes in which participation is required, these are usually "active participation" (asking questions, commenting, including information from readings or examples). "Participation" may include asking questions or commenting. "Not participating" might include not attending class, talking or texting on a cell phone. Whatever your requirements, make your students aware of these and be fair. For online classes, postings or replies have more stringent requirements of proper grammar, citations, organization and so forth. Using a rubric, you can mark your scale in each category or can assign point values in each category. Make sure you include the rubric with your syllabus or in the course website.

Example: In this example, the initial post is worth 5 points with each criterion of the post having equal value. The points can be adjusted in each category as needed so the maximum number of points is 5. Additional description can be included in each category. A student may have excellent examples but good in other categories; the total point value would be 4.5.

	Excellent	Good	Poor
Organization	1	.5	0
Specific examples	1	.5	0
Analysis	1	.5	0
Citation/reference	1	.5	0
Grammar/spelling	1	.5	0

3. Read papers twice: once for clarity, organization, argument; once for mechanics. While this seems repetitive, reading papers twice focuses your mind on different requirements of the paper. The first reading can be organization, content, etc. This is the heart of the paper; you can determine a student's depth of writing and research. Then you can read for mechanics including verb tenses, sentence structure (fragments and run-ons), correct citation formatting, spelling and such. If we try to tackle all requirements in one sitting, we easily get sidetracked about rewording sentences or spelling errors and do not focus on the argument and content. A rubric is great to use for grading papers. A hard copy rubric can be used for each on campus paper (hard copy) and you can check each category as you read. For online papers, the rubric can be a document or template you can mark.

4. Be constructive. Noting a grade of "B" without feedback does not help the student to improve for future papers. Do not merely criticize the paper, provide positive and constructive comments. These comments might include information about the quotes used, research sources, word usage, or a comment about a particularly excellent paragraph. If you use a rubric, this is much easier for students to understand.

5. Paper grading programs. Paper grading programs can be useful. These are not "automatic" programs that scan and grade papers. You must still read each paper.

Grading programs can speed the process by inserting specific comments. In most of these programs, you set your cursor at the location for your comment, then choose from a drop down menu of preset comments. This makes grading papers much faster, especially if students are prone to certain grammatical mistakes. You do not type "incorrect verb tense" 20 times throughout the paper – insert from the drop down menu. Some programs also provide examples and suggestions for students; I find this helpful in passive/active voice. There are several grading programs available, including the program in Turnitin, and Grade Assist, T.A. Toolbar, Essay Tagger. Depending upon the program, a score is dedicated to each category (as determined by the instructor or college).

If you do not want to purchase or use a grading program, you can use a voice recognition program or macros that let you insert your comments into the paper. A voice recognition program can be helpful if you have specific content or comments for student papers (and if you are tired of typing comments). Macros are set by you in word process programs (Microsoft Word); when you strike a key, a specific comment is inserted into the paper. For online or on campus classes, students upload the paper to the class website (or send to me by email). I download papers and correct/comment using the review-track changes option. I can use voice recognition or macros.

Are "automatic" programs available so you can scan the paper and let the computer program score this for you? Yes. However, to accurately score a submitted paper, sample papers at each grade score must be submitted to "program" the scoring criteria. Needless to say, if you are teaching one class with 30 students this would be time consuming and not practical, because you would need prior graded papers in order to grade this set of papers. Also, the auto-grade programs often cannot distinguish analogy or synthesis. For large universities that have thousands of students and that can afford such programs, this might be an option. However, for the lone faculty the cost and time would probably be prohibitive.

6. Voice recognition software. Voice recognition software can be useful for grading student papers, composing lectures, or composing syllabi. With a voice recognition software, you can load the program onto your computer or laptop and directly dictate

your lesson plan into the computer. I set the cursor at the location, then speak my comment. I can provide concise information and suggestions for student writings.   There are several voice recognition software programs available. If you have Microsoft Office, this is available (free) in the software package. You just need to buy a microphone and activate and test. Other voice recognition programs include Dragon Naturally/Dragon Dictate, SpeechGear, and more! I am not recommending any particular voice recognition software – do some research to find the best for your computer, classes, and uses.

7. Organize your student submissions. If you require students to submit online to a drop box or email, requiring students to submit files named in a specific format will save time in locating and shifting through student papers.

> Students usually save a paper by its title. However if the paper topic is similar, then the papers submitted will have similar titles. You will receive 30 papers titled "Roman Empire", then you will download these (either individually or on batch), then either return to the student individually by email or change name of the document and upload as a batch. If you return each paper after grading, you do not need to change the document name. But think about the save-click/review-click/save-click/ access   email-click/student   name-click/upload-

click/send-click. Yipes! Way too much time for this.

There is a reason Henry Ford's assembly line worked – it is efficient! I suggest to download student papers as a batch, then grade, then upload as a batch.

I ask students to save their papers in the following format: last name_firstname_assignmentnumber. This would be: Macek_Jo_Paper2. This would not be the paper title but the "save as" document title. I download papers as a batch, grade, then return (upload) as a batch. This is much easier and faster. This also works for on-campus classes. You can save papers to a computer file, grade, then return to students.

8. <u>Multiple choice tests/quizzes.</u> Tests are one type of assessment. Like papers and other assessments (discussion questions, activities) test questions should relate to the course objectives. While students think tests are wicked, perhaps even "evil," and are really an instructor's form of revenge, I like tests and quizzes for two reasons.

Periodic testing forces students to study the course material. Instructors know that review and repetition is important to learn material. The more students discuss, repeat, and analyze the material the better students understand the material.

While a few students might state they "never study but still pass" tests, these students have learned the test taking techniques that include memorization, critical thinking, and analysis. In addition, these students may come to your class with some pre-knowledge of the subject matter. Or they research information on the internet, scan fellow student's lecture notes or read Cliff's Notes. Or they were able to do this in high school, but college is a "whole new ballgame." (As students progress in their classes, they will need to sharpen their study skills and enhance their research techniques – you and I know this and your students will discover this soon enough.)

Testing provides the student - and you - feedback about learning. A student can (and should) analyze his/her score and determine why certain answers were wrong or right: poor recall of material, not enough study time, poor testing techniques. Scores can also provide feedback to you about your students and also the pace of material covered in class. If the majority of students scored low, then perhaps the you can offer supplemental information, additional resources, referral to tutoring services, or a different approach to the material. We may understand the information with our years of experience, but students may have a difficult time grasping concepts.

9. <u>Make testing easy on yourself.</u> Many textbooks include instructor test banks. In many cases, questions can be randomly taken from the test bank – by chapter or unit or entire book. Do not choose questions just to have questions – make sure these conform to your course objectives.

10. <u>Use bubble-type (Scantron) answer sheets.</u> A fill-in-the-bubble answer sheet is much faster to grade than a test on which students circle or write the answer. Scantron is a bubble sheet/program used by some colleges. A master answer form is scanned through the Scantron machine, then student forms are scanned and scored.

I worked at a vocational college that did not have a Scantron, so I made my own fill-in-the-bubble answer sheet in Excel. The a-b-c-d multiple choice options were at the top then bubbles (squares) under each letter. (True/false can be a-b). I made a master answer template by cutting out the correct answer, then I placed the master answer sheet over student sheet and mark answers. Low tech, yes, but efficient and faster than the quick eye-dart method of master-student sheet.

11. Keep your tests secure. If you re-use tests, keep the master or copies in areas not accessible by others. Unfortunately, some students believe that test scores are more important than integrity and they will do almost anything to get that good grade – including cheating, lying, and stealing.

I suggest to keep hard copies of tests and CD-ROM's of instructor test banks in locked file drawers. These should be locked even if you are in your office; you probably step out for coffee or such and leave your filing cabinets unlocked. Do not do this!

Likewise, the testing area should be secure. Students should remove all materials from desks, including backpacks, books, water bottles, cell phones, purses. You do not know the information being passed if a student looks a his/her cell phone. I tell students to turn their cell phones "off" not vibrate.

12. Review tests with students. Tests are not just grades, they are learning experiences for students. When students can analyze the reasons for their responses they can evaluate their study habits, testing techniques, or refocus on course content. If your policy is

no-review, then tell students what you will (may) focus on. This is the time to utilize your graduate students – they can meet with students or explain the relevant information to students. Remember that human beings cannot memorize textbooks and few people have eidetic memories. Also, your tests might emphasize certain points but papers and activities might emphasize other objectives.

13. Use campus services. Your college may have services for you and your students to help with testing or grading. This might be copy services that can copy tests or clerks or graduate assistants who can score tests to faculty development offices that host workshops about teaching, testing, and assessment. As instructors, we want to be in charge of our classes and in control. However, using support services does not mean that we give up our control to others; we can ask for assistance yet still be in control of our course content and focus.

14. Formative assessments can help students as well as you. A formative assessment is an evaluation conducted during the course but which is not graded. In other words, assessing while the information is "forming" in students' minds. This is usually not a formal "test" but an activity or exercise or questioning. This gives you information about whether your students are learning.

> I usually use "impromptu" group activities as a formative assessment. After a lecture of the topic, I divide students into small groups of 3 or 4 and

give them with a worksheet or scenario or questions to discuss. I can monitor each group and provide comments and direction. Students then share information with the entire class. This works well with smaller class sizes – up to about 40 or so.

15. Summative assessments can help students as well as you. A summative assessment in a final evaluation about the topic(s) you presented. This is often an exam covering a set of chapters, or perhaps a paper that requires analysis or in-depth examination.

ADDITIONAL RESOURCES

Babb, D., & Mirabella, J. (2007). *Make money teaching online.*
　　Hoboken: Wiley & Sons.

Berg, G. A. (2005). *Lessons from the edge.* Westport, CT: Praeger
　　Publishers.

Boettcher, J. V. & Conrad, R. M. (2004). *Faculty guide for moving
　　teaching and learning to the web.* 2nd Edition. Phoenix, AZ:
　　League for Innovation.

Brookfield, S. D. (1990). *The skillful teacher.* San Franscico:
　　Jossey-Bass.

Brown, R. (2007). *How to teach online.* USA: Lulu.

Fleming, D. (2009). *Teaching workshops effectively.* Chandler,
　　AZ: Infinite Wisdom Press.

Goodyear, P. (2002). *Psychological foundations for networked
　　learning. Networked learning: perspectives and issues.*
　　New York: Springer-Verlag.

Greive, D. (201). *A handbook for adjunct & part-Time faculty & teachers of adults.* Elyria, OH: Info-Tec.

Jackson, R. R. (2009). *Never work harder than your students.* Alexandria, VA: ASCD.

Macek, J. (2009, September). *Discussion management tips for online educators.* Retrieved from eLearn Magazine: www.elearnmag.acm.org/featured.cfm?aid=162115.

Macek, J. (2013, January). *7 student myths of the online classroom.* Retrieved from eLearn Magazine: www.elearnmag.acm.org/archive.cfm?aid=2429654.

Pelz, B. (2004). (My) Three principles of effective online pedagogy. *JALN (Journal of Asynchronous Learning Networks)* 8(3). www.sloan-c.org/publications/jaln/v8n3/v8n3_pelz.asp.

Whitaker, T. (2004). *What great teachers do differently.* Larchmont, NY: Eye On Education.

Helpful Software

This is a very short and certainly not comprehensive list of helpful technology. There are hundreds of software programs available for presentations, composing videos, grading papers, and voice recognition. Read the user and consumer reviews for programs. Talk to people. Research programs that are useful for you in your teaching situation. By the time this book is published I am sure that dozens of software products will be on the market.

CustomShow – slide show presentation

Dragon NaturallySpeaking – voice recognition

EasyTagger – paper grading

Grabilla - screenshot

GradeAssist – paper grading

Greenshot - screenshot

Jing – screenshot

Microsoft Media – slide show presentation/media presentation

PowerPoint – slide show presentation

Prezi – slide show presentation

TA Toolbar – paper grading

Author Profile

Ms. Macek has over 20 years of experience in college teaching and administration and is devoted to helping students achieve their educational goals and faculty to become better teachers.

Jo Macek earned a Master's in Teaching from Wayne State University in Detroit, Michigan in 1991. She earned additional graduate and undergraduate credit in instructional technology, history, political science, and Spanish.

Ms. Macek worked as an administrator in higher education, high school teacher, museum administrator, vocational counselor in a substance abuse facility, and college faculty.

She was published in eLearn Magazine, "Collections: A Journal for Museum and Archives Professionals", Women and Politics Encyclopedia and presented at Microcomputers in Education, Arizona Career Technical Conference, and The University of Michigan Annual People of Color Conference.

Ms. Macek has over 20 years of experience in college teaching and administration and is devoted to helping students achieve their educational goals and faculty to become better teachers.

Comments may be directed to:

jtmacek@gmail.com

Forever Publishing LLC

Independent publisher of fiction and non-fiction.

www.foreverpublishing.net

Casa Grande, Arizona

Job Search Aids

This is a short list of sites to search for potential jobs in college teaching.

Academic360.com

Academiccareers.com

Adjunctnation.com

Adjunctopia.com

Adjunctprofessorjobs.com

CareerBuilder.com

Chronicle of Higher Education

Collegesanduniversities.us

Geteducated.com

Higheredjobs.com

Insidehighered.com

Indeed.com

LinkedIn.com

Onlineadjunctjobs.blogspot.com

Onlinecollges.net

Simplyhired.com

Twitter.com

Utexas.edu/world/univ/state

* 9 7 8 0 9 8 9 1 2 9 0 2 2 *